D1495308

LITTLE BLACK
RACING BOOK

LITTLE BLACK RACING BOOK

The Inside Track on Horse Racing

TONY STAFFORD
OF
The Daily Telegraph

FOREWORD BY LESTER PIGGOTT

CollinsWillow
An Imprint of HarperCollins*Publishers*

First published in 1994 by
CollinsWillow
an imprint of HarperCollins*Publishers*
London

© Tony Stafford 1994

All rights reserved. No part of this publication may be
reproduced, stored in a retrieval system, or transmitted,
in any form or by any means, electronic, mechanical,
photocopying, recording or otherwise, without the
prior written permission of the publishers.

**A CIP catalogue record for this book is
available from the British Library**

ISBN 0 00 218477 X

Printed and bound in Great Britain by
Butler & Tanner Ltd, Frome and London

Contents

For my wife Gill who has endured more than 25 years of my obsession with racing. Her 25th wedding anniversary was spent at the races this July and her wedding was delayed until 4 p.m. because the Eclipse Stakes was being run that day at Sandown.

Foreword

by Lester Piggott

PEOPLE WHO ARE ABLE to earn their living doing something they like are very lucky. As the following pages show, Tony Stafford has made his hobby into his living, and the fun he has had from his work in racing shines through in this book.

Not all racing journalists, or any other journalists, for that matter, can be trusted to print exactly what they are told. Tony does not misquote, and that is part of the reason I agreed to write for him my story of why I was returning to riding when I made my comeback.

Some papers said I did not write that story, but as you will read here, I did, and enjoyed doing it. It was nice to prove that you are not finished when you are over fifty, and I think my comeback helped other middle-aged people real-ize they still had a lot to offer. Experience and knowing your job from years of doing it are just as valuable as youth and fitness. Tony shows here that his twenty-five years in racing have given him a wide range of experience in many coun-tries. He has put it to use in advising owners and trainers on aspects of racing, as the book shows.

When you are a jockey looking for rides that can win, you

need to know what's happening, and the same thing goes for tipsters. It is not easy to win the *Sporting Life* naps' table. To win it once you can be lucky. To win it twice you need a little more than just luck. You need to be well connected and work at it. Over twenty-five years, Tony has worked hard at racing and has enjoyed the benefits. I think you will enjoy reading about it.

Newmarket, July 1994

Acknowledgements

ALTHOUGH SOME OF the events described in these pages occurred before I joined the *Daily Telegraph* in January 1972, most of the remainder would never have happened without the paper's help.

I was lucky enough to benefit from an unexpected vacancy on the racing desk, very much on the recommendation of the paper's then deputy racing editor, Noel Blunt, a Yorkshireman whose capacity to cause mirth when he later became the *Sporting Life*'s chief sub-editor, blessed as he was with a penchant for malapropisms, was exceeded only by his innate helpfulness. It was Noel who, when the desk was puzzled by John Oaksey's use of the term Krugerrands in one article, suggested: 'Ask Tony, he knows Latin!' Among other things, this book gives me a chance to record my thanks to someone who really did change my fortunes.

In those days two more Yorkshiremen, the late Kingsley Wright, whose rule by fear disguised a soft centre, and the recently (in 1993) remarried Bob Glendinning, were sports editor and racing editor respectively. Bob inadvertently sparked one memorable winning gamble on the day he retired in April 1979. We'd had an ante-post bet on Tommy Carmody being champion jump jockey, and had already given up, whereupon Bob stumped up his tenner. There was still time on that Friday night to back the last winner at Liverpool, Anna's Prince at 15–2, and I followed it with £25 each way on Rubstic at 28–1 in the Grand National the next day – a winner I passed on to my BBC Radio London listeners the same morning.

During eleven years as the *Telegraph*'s racing editor, I worked first with Kingsley and then with the talented Ted Barrett before the advent of David Welch, himself a notable tipster who napped Snow Knight for his then paper the *Leicester Mercury* at 50–1 in the 1974 Derby. David's foresight and meticulous planning have taken the *Daily Telegraph*'s sports section into a different league from its competitors.

Remarkably few changes occurred on the desk in those years, although my closest friend George Hill, in five years during which he spent as much time selling horses and doing phantom tipping shifts on the *Daily Express* as a substitute Bendex, was one non-stayer. As a full-time bloodstock agent George's notable acquisitions included Bajan Sunshine the day before his Cesarewitch win and the Italian Classic winner Atoll from Robert Sangster. He could also tell you of the deals that got away (including Dr Devious); but now, as jockey's agent for Walter Swinburn and the apprentice David McCabe, his considerable abilities are being properly stretched.

The present *Telegraph* racing team has been bolstered by the addition of Marcus Armytage, whose first few months suggest that he will be a fine replacement for Lord Oaksey, who naturally gets more in the paper now than when he was actually working on it!

The men on the desk rarely get many plaudits, but if it's a safe pair of hands you want, at Canary Wharf there are six pairs. Racing editor Adrian Hunt's diffident manner disguises a shrewd understanding of the racing game, and over twenty-five years, first at the *Greyhound Express*, which he joined straight from school, and then at the *Daily Telegraph*, his reliability has been a watchword. His deputy Danny Coupland adds a straightforward honesty and ability to cut through the baggage and home in on the essence of a story. You'd come up with an idea and put it to Danny, who'd say: 'It's a great idea, but who'd be interested in it?' Ninety-nine times out of a hundred his news sense will be right; and there would be no more reliable ally.

Kevin Perry brings the experience of working on weekly racing papers and a spell on the Press Association to his input. Quick-thinking, alert, Kevin is also a great time expert and I always think it's a pity there's not really scope for using his time handicap in the paper. Mike Roberts, another weekly paper man, has also spent many years as a racecourse reporter on the *Sporting Life* and keeps his own scrapbook of racing stories, always being able to put his hands on the relevant piece when a deadline approaches and I need some background. If Brian Matthews will never be happy that he missed winning the British Open, he can rest assured that he is the world champion on racing page detail. His scrutiny of the racecards, form figures and other important sections of the page ensures few errors the following morning.

Finally, Steve Dillon adds his own speciality. He is a great statistics man for the big day and in a perfect world there would always be room for his facts and figures on the Derby, Grand National and other major events. Steve's father Mick was a stalls handler and grandfather Bernard, a great jockey, was once consort to the singer Marie Lloyd.

A fine team. No wonder it's all been such fun.

A New Dawn

DURING THE FINAL STAGES of writing this book (indeed, when the copy should already have been with the editors) an event of cataclysmic proportions occurred with a whisper and changed the entire face of racing in the immediate future.

Like the Berlin Wall and communism in Russia, monoliths which they thought could never be shifted, opposition to racing and betting on Sundays was effectively stifled and the prohibition ended by a shrewd politician noticing a chink of opportunity in a parliamentary bill on Sunday trading.

Jim Paice MP, whose constituency includes part of Newmarket, the horse-racing capital of the world, was the alert individual who in one move enabled racing in Britain to compete on level terms with its European counterparts – and also with other British sports which have simply ignored legal constraints to proceed on Sundays.

In July a list of twenty-four Sunday fixtures was issued for 1995, two on each of twelve dates, beginning in May when the Madagans One Thousand Guineas at Newmarket will become the first Sunday Classic. Betting shops will be open and there seems no doubt that eventually a Sunday Derby will be the aim – although in 1995 it is expected to be staged on the Saturday.

The biggest benefit should be that families will be encouraged to attend. But, as you will see if you read on, pricing policies at the various courses will need to change if a day out for four is not to prove prohibitively expensive. Still, it's a start. Welcome to the twenty-first century, racing; and thanks, Mr Paice.

Glorious Uncertainty

THE LONGER YOU are involved in horse racing, whether as journalist, owner, trainer, jockey or merely the smallest betting-shop follower, the more you realize there's never a time when you know as much as you need to know. Even people like Lester Piggott, with his string of riding titles and record number of Classic wins, a man who has been at the top of his profession for more than forty years, can be surprised at the outcome of a particular race, at seeing a horse he thought would win fail, or a no-hoper come in first. It is precisely this uncertainty, and the conflict of opinion that goes with it, which has made horse racing the pre-eminent betting medium, and which has been a constant feature of the sport's development, from its basest form when rich men pitted their own champions against their contemporaries' best horses, to the scrupulously regulated industry of the present day.

In short, for many people, it really does matter which horse wins. For the owner of the Derby winner, for the newspaper tipster who finds the good-priced handicap winner and for the ten-pence punter who aims to win a few

15

pounds on an outsider, the daily racing programme offers opportunities for profit and, most of all, for fun.

Looking back on a career in racing journalism that has spanned more than twenty-five years, I would have to say that even the losing days can offer enjoyment, while the winning ones sometimes bring euphoria. But transcending victory and defeat, the spectacle, the true competitiveness and the professionalism of so many disparate talents combine to make the 'glorious uncertainty' precisely that.

Birth of a racing man

Just as apparently random as anything you might see on the track are the circumstances that pitchfork you into a certain activity in the first place, it seems. How did I, for instance, born in Hackney in London's East End, gravitate to writing about horse racing for a living, sometimes even tipping the odd winner? None of my friends from the early days did anything of the sort. The odd college lecturer emerged, an accountant or two and, no doubt, if one followed the trail back to the early 1950s, a few safe-crackers and market traders as well.

Mention of the early 1950s does have a point to it. Those were formative years when we stood at the Clock End at Highbury to watch Arsenal, gathered in the cheap seats at The Oval or Lord's to watch Peter May or Denis Compton, and suffered excruciatingly slow coach journeys to Kempton Park on Easter Monday, to Hurst Park at – was it Whitsun? – and on cold mornings in early spring to the Craven and Guineas meetings in Newmarket.

The 1950s may now seem innocent and far away but for a

sports enthusiast they provided plentiful opportunity (through the radio especially) to assimilate information and lay down a bedrock on which later experience could thrive. Details, statistics, famous names, both human and equine, swilled around in a maelstrom, and the popular radio personality Leslie Welch, the 'Memory Man', was a role model for youthful imitators. Why else should I still remember Arsenal line-ups in 1955 or recall an hour's batting for Middlesex at The Oval in which Denis Compton and his partner Peter Delisle managed just three runs?

Who Delisle was and where he went afterwards are not part of that memory. Images of trips to the racetrack, though, are. In those days of the late fifties we would catch the charabanc (coach to you) at Clapton Pond, one of several stops before it took the old A11 north towards Newmarket. Nowadays, thanks to motorways, the drive would probably take you an hour and a quarter. Then, it was a much longer haul on the bus, necessitating a stop at halfway − presumably at Saffron Walden.

Occasionally we used to have a celebrity on the coach. Racetracks in the south, both before the war and in the first fifteen years after it, were graced by an Indian-born tipster who gloried in the self-styled title of Prince Monolulu and whose catch-phrase 'I've gotta horse' enticed silver coinage from many a believer. His information was presumably little better or worse than anyone else's, but his presentation compared favourably with the more furtive style of the home-bred touts, and he prospered (a little) accordingly. Until the next race at least.

One particular incident that has lodged in the brain from these years, hardly memorable in itself, revolves around an Easter foray to Kempton Park. Compared with Hackney,

17

Sunbury and Hampton Court were a different planet. On the big days, massive crowds from everywhere in the south-east converged on the course. As you travel from the grand-stand end at Kempton nowadays, there's a tall wooden fence which stretches right to the end of the Jubilee Course, ten furlongs away. The coaches came from the other direction, and I recall sitting in a massive traffic jam, consisting almost entirely of coaches, inching towards the enclosure.

So large were the crowds in the 1950s that we were housed in the old Course enclosure, paying probably 2s 6d to go in. Kempton has changed less than some of the other major tracks, apart from a new building at the paddock end. The old Silver Ring is still in use – and is often regarded as 'too good' in that it extends to about half a furlong from the finish; and the old stand remains, a little sadly, at the entrance to the straight.

The first race we saw that day marked another stage in my racing education. It was a mile maiden, and as the field passed our cramped position, my dad's horse was leading. When they announced the result, with his horse nowhere, I realized that quite a lot can happen in the last two and a half furlongs of any race.

There is a postscript to this story, too. At Kempton on Easter Monday 1994 I resolved to walk down to the old stand, which nowadays during the summer houses the birch from the hurdles and fences for the jumps track. I stood and watched one race amid the quiet. Coming back to the main stands, I bumped into Tim Nelligan, Chairman of United Racecourses, and David Hillyard, boss of Racecourse Holdings Trust, which had just acquired United Racecourses and its three tracks, Kempton, Sandown Park and Epsom. Nelligan, who always seems a mite surprised at my affection for Kempton (I once owned a horse who won there by twenty lengths in a Flat race on Easter Monday) said that in the old days they could accommodate 55,000 there. No wonder it took so long to get in.

'A licence to print money'

My generation grew up with betting shops. Our parents either went to the races, patronized a street bookie or opened an account with a credit firm. But the first betting shops that opened at the start of the 1960s, a time which coincided with the fertilization of the dormant seeds of my interest in racing, made it possible for anyone to have a cash bet and collect the winnings within a few minutes of the 'weighed-in' signal.

Compared with the glossy high street emporia of today's Big Three firms, Ladbrokes, William Hill and Coral, the old shops were one-man outfits, with only the most basic facilities, offering inaccurate commentaries and minimal information to their clients. It wasn't long, however, before comments by such prominent bookmakers as the Glasgow-based John Banks, whose oft-quoted maxim that betting shops were 'a licence to print money' was so prophetic, encouraged the big combines to enter and transform the field.

In the early days there was no tax or duty on bets; bookmakers paid one-third the odds for a place (first and second) in five- to seven-horse races and a quarter the odds a place (one-two-three) in any other race. My own betting, technically illegal until March 1964 when I turned eighteen, could at times be highly profitable, even if it was a little speculative. I had a friend, much more circumspect than myself, who specialized in backing second favourites each way in five-horse races when the favourite was odds-on. Often he'd be on a 3–1 shot, when the third favourite might be as long as 8–1 or more. Most times, the second favourite would dutifully follow the market leader home, in which case my pal would get his each-way stake back. Less often, but on a significant number of occasions, his horse would win, and he regularly subsidized his weekend activities with these easily earned profits. Needless to say, the present-day bunch of bookmakers have long since expunged such opportunities, restricting place betting to a fifth of the win odds, or even a sixth in certain instances.

Missing the break?

A few years later, in the short period between A levels and my first journalistic job as a trainee on the *Walthamstow Guardian*, I was on the way to work one Saturday morning, resigned to the fact that the Sandown meeting later that day was bound to be abandoned because of the weather. The bus from Tottenham to Dalston Junction passed one betting shop just before my destination, and from the upstairs window I fleetingly caught sight through the glass of the shop of the word 'Sandown', but maddeningly the bottom of the glass obscured whatever was written underneath. There was another shop just around the corner where I had to catch a second bus to Clapton and there, hardly surprisingly, the news that Sandown had indeed fallen victim to the elements was received with much regret.

As I was about to leave the shop, though, I noticed an

apparently redundant page of the *Sporting Life*, closer inspection of which revealed a meeting in Ireland at the now long defunct Mullingar course. I decided to risk two pounds, relying on the tips in the paper. As all the tipsters seemed agreed in every race, it looked potentially a good day for favourites – small fields, heavy going and the like. So, taking my life in my hands, I settled on a win accumulator on the favourites in all six races. Two pounds down the drain by any calculations.

The afternoon's *Grandstand* viewing, however, became rather interesting when the results began to trickle through. The first three favourites all won, 6–4, 3–1 and believe it or not, 4–1 (maybe not in that order). My calculations quickly made that a hundred pounds going on, and when the next two went in, both at short prices, there was only the bumper to worry about.

Irish bumper races – National Hunt races with no jumps – have been the traditional proving ground for future jumpers, and this particular event was almost certainly going to be a one-horse race. 'They always know what's going to win them,' was my simplistic self delusion. My prospects, however, were made rather more complicated by a last betting show in which two horses were disputing favouritism at 7–4 and 9–4.

In those days there were no commentaries from Ireland and when the result was announced, the horse which had been second favourite was named first. It seemed that an age then passed before the starting prices were given – to reveal that the winner was 2–1 joint favourite!

The postscript to this tale is rather more mundane. That night, along with the regular crowd of former schoolmates, I took my £380 winnings along to Clapton dog track and subsequently had to decline the prospect of a late night in the West End on the grounds of penury. It had all gone into the satchels.

Around that time I had started working in a local shop on Saturdays and during the evenings to settle bets left during the afternoon. At one time I was offered a free partnership when one of the three partners decided to retire, but opted instead for newspapers. I've never stopped wondering whether it was the right choice. As the man said, 'It's a licence to print money.'

CHAPTER TWO

The Ring, the Book – and the Tote

THERE ARE MANY racegoers who would never dream of placing a bet on a race, and a larger group whose gambling never exceeds the minimum stake allowed on the Tote. These distinct categories apart, high among most people's reasons for going to the track, or especially to the betting shop, is to place a bet. The whole business of racing owes its existence to that willingness to wager on the outcome of races.

A simple enough scenario, perhaps; but British racing in the 1990s has become rather more complicated. Horse racing has been conducted seriously on these shores for more than 300 years, but in the last thirty, since the inception of betting shops and their development into the relatively lavish emporia of the present era, technological advance has altered every aspect of the sport, including – perhaps especially – betting on it.

Punch drunk on pictures

There is no doubt that technology has a lot to answer for. Satellite Information Services (SIS) have clearly transformed the off-course environment for racing fans over a few short years by sending film of non-televised races into betting shops, but the avarice of the bookmaking chains has turned a welcome facility into too much of a good thing. Often in the periods when jump and Flat racing go in tandem, in spring and autumn, the proliferation of race meetings becomes almost bewildering. Five, six or seven fixtures are paraded before the hapless shop viewer and, as if these regular bits of equine action were not enough, they will be punctuated every ten minutes or so by supplementary action from two greyhound tracks. Indeed, on Saturdays, there can be two morning dog cards of fourteen races each; then some selected races from the main meeting in South Africa; and then the diet of afternoon horse racing, followed by evening action.

All this layering of indigestible fare makes a day in the betting shop rather like a slow-moving roulette wheel, where the sole object is to rid the customer of his money. The sight of the lemming-like rush (I do it myself sometimes) to get on as the 'off' signal is sounded must make betting-shop staff marvel at the idiocy of the run-of-the-mill punter.

Playing the market

A real growth area in recent years has been spread betting, which basically adapts the principle of stock market activity to betting on sports, including horse racing.

In its simplest form, a spread bet is a two-way wager between the bookmaker and the gambler on a specific situation. How many winners will (for instance) Frankie Dettori ride in a season? How many points will England's rugby team score? How many runs will Brian Lara chalk up in a season for Warwickshire? The bookmaker's job is to select a range of results in such cases, on which there will be disparate opinion. Some punters will believe the outcome of the situation will be above and others below the stated numerical range. Punters are therefore asked to buy (believe the outcome will be above the higher number) or sell (if taking the opposite view). Sporting Index, with their highly presentable representative Wally Pyrah, lead the field in this type of betting. Large winnings (and losses) are possible; naturally, there is a spread, which should ensure profitable trading over a period.

Trust, plastic and balancing the books

Even the old-established ways of betting have taken on new forms. Traditionally, credit betting was undertaken on the basis of regular settling on both sides. Such bets were not recoverable in law, so a far from healthy proportion of potential profits for many bookmakers just disappeared when punters simply refused to pay.

Some of the major firms have been keen to change over to debit betting by way of Switch- and Delta-backed debit cards. Here the punter is effectively betting in cash rather than on credit, as the card company has to authorize each bet before it is confirmed.

The attractions of debit betting for the bookmaker are clear: there's no risk of the punter disappearing, and less need to monitor whether a client is too far beyond his credit limit. However, one major credit firm, Victor Chandler, run by one of the most adventurous bookmakers from a family steeped in the business, began debit card betting but soon abandoned it. The time-lag in placing and acceptance of bets caused frequent problems for people accustomed to instant verification, and in the case of prices altering either up or down during that time-lag, there is the scope for irritation on the part of punter and bookmaker alike. Victor Chandler found that the flexible friend became a rather inflexible irritant.

My own experience of betting accounts has been singularly unsuccessful. Credit betting requires a disciplined approach and there is always the tendency towards injudicious staking. In my own case, a smallish initial stake was inevitably lost, and the following series of bets became increasingly speculative, aimed merely at getting the said account into parity. Thankfully, others find it easier to manage their betting more sensibly.

Comfort in the familiar – at a price

One of the more striking aspects of racecourse facilities in recent years has been the development of the on-course betting shops. Until 1992, these shops were nearly all operated by a bookmaking conglomerate known as NARBOL, which offered facilities and betting opportunities far inferior to those available in high street shops. Then Southwell's enlightened boss Ron Muddle decided not to renew

NARBOL's licence to operate the shop at his track, giving Ian Storey-Moore, a local bookmaker and also a former England soccer international who used to play for Nottingham Forest, the opportunity to take over the licence.

Storey-Moore had only hours to organize the change-over and the former occupiers of the shop threatened legal action to reverse the decision. Muddle stood firm; Storey-Moore still has the Southwell shop, and this single action – at the time widely regarded as a foolhardy move on the part of Muddle and his son Richard, who now runs Wolverhampton racecourse – became the model for the dismantling of NARBOL's on-course empire.

The Tote's off-course division also operated some of the shops; they have generally retained non-exclusive contracts, notably at some of the major southern tracks. Now they share sites with their high street competitors.

Corals, Ladbrokes and Hills each have a stake in this side of the business, and their on-course shops are just as lavish as the best high street branches. In general, they offer the same facilities as they can off-course, with the single exception that bets on the meeting at which the shop is based are settled at starting price, so as not to compete over-favourably with the course bookmakers.

Strangely, the day-to-day betting-shop punter seems unable totally to kick the habit of betting-shop action when he goes to the track, for the on-course outlets are extremely well attended – much to the satisfaction of the tracks, who enjoy a significant rake-off. The punters seem to be content with paying just 5 or 6 per cent deductions, compared with 10 per cent in their usual betting shop off-course; and yet, in an activity where margins must be important, it does seem odd that many punters ignore the chance to bet totally free of tax a few yards away from the shop in the open air with a course bookmaker.

Tote versus book

There are times when the financial structure of racing convinces otherwise unbiased individuals that the absence of the major bookmaking firms, and their penchant for skimming the cream off the betting public's vast fund of cash, would be helpful for the sport. But then, at the track, the alternative, a pool monopoly, often looks a far less tempting prospect. In many instances Tote prices, because of the fixed deduction, compare most unfavourably with bookmakers' odds, and the biggest turn-off of all is the inability to strike a bet at a definite price.

Take a dull, ill-attended day at a midlands track. You fancy an outsider and place a £20 bet on the Tote, attracted by the current price of 50–1 shown on the screen. Thirty seconds later, with your bet logged into the system, the odds will have shrunk to 5–1 if you are lucky. Of course, as Tote Direct takes a bigger hold, bringing more off-course money into the equation, those minuscule pools will become a rarity, but it is still inadvisable to place even modestly strong bets on the Tote at the smaller tracks.

My own favourite time to bet on the Tote is at the major meetings like Royal Ascot or the Cheltenham Festival. The stands are crammed with racegoers, many of whom can easily get to a Tote terminal but find the prospect of going through the scrum to the bookmakers, which in each case are a fair way from the Members' stand, most unappealing. Both meetings are the province of the invitee, the once-a-year racegoer whose knowledge of the racing game is, understandably, sketchy. At Ascot in June, for example, just a few jockeys will be familiar, with Carson, Eddery, Dettori and Piggott all registering high scores on the recognition scale; consequently, all the horses ridden by these household names will be at much shorter odds on the Tote than in the betting ring, especially in races like the Royal Hunt Cup where the bookmakers in any case enjoy trimming the odds themselves. But outside that coterie of top jockeys, the converse is true. With massive pools on each race, the shrewd punter has ample time to compare odds, but in thirty-runner races like the Hunt Cup or the Wokingham Stakes, *most* horses will be much longer prices on the machine, with the outsiders coming in at up to 500–1 when the largest starting price of any of the runners rarely exceeds 50–1.

Examples of this trend are regularly available; one from the 1993 Royal Ascot meeting, the King George V Handicap, a race for three-year-olds over a mile and a half, will emphasize the point nicely. The race went to Learmont, owned by Sheikh Mohammed and trained by John Gosden, a colt that had won his previous race in a Sandown maiden, and hardly from an unfashionable source. That was reflected in his starting price of 14–1 in a field of sixteen. What was unfashionable, and unattractive from the point of view of the hordes being entertained in the Grandstand boxes, was the jockey. John Carroll might be a leading northern-based rider and the regular partner of Jack Berry's flotilla of winning horses, but his southern forays had been rare considering that he had reached his half century in each of the previous five years. However, Carroll has been employed by Gosden for a number of northern wins over the past few years. When Learmont won, his Tote backers will have been delighted with a payout of more than 26–1.

The best thing about Tote betting, even if the odds are often a little smaller than the bookies', is the rapidity of the payout. Often a race will be keenly contested. If the stewards fail to spot an incident immediately, for instance if the horses tighten up in the closing stages, it is wise to present a winning ticket for payment promptly. Even if technically it is unfair to pull a fast one on this august government-licensed body before confirmation of the result, there have been instances where the Tote has had to pay out on two horses.

There is a rider to this point. One day in 1993 at Leicester – why was I betting on the Tote on an ill-attended winter day in the midlands? – I watched my horse fade as an outsider romped home, and, like everyone else on the track, threw away my ticket. Then it was announced there was no winner, so all stakes would be refunded. Having vainly scrabbled around on the ground in the area close to where I dumped the ticket, I returned to the window at which I had placed my bet, and was actually remembered by the nice lady who had processed the ticket (there aren't that many grey, fat, ageing optimists around). The supervisor gently told me that as other people were in the same boat, I would have to write to Tote House, tell them where the bet had been placed, on which horse and to what stake, and in the course of time I would probably be reimbursed.

Probably is a massive word in life, and looms even larger in the much more serious activity of horse racing. I was first advised that I would have to wait for the auditors to peruse the day's accounts. Needless to say, seven weeks after the race, I got a polite note regretting that in fact my bet had been presented in the normal way, so I would not get my money back. Fair enough. Any fool knows that you should keep your ticket until you are absolutely sure of a dividend being declared.

That's true. But there's nothing more galling than getting home after a bad day at the races and emptying your pockets to find no more than a clutch of small change and a bunch of losing Tote or bookmakers' tickets. That's why the punters screw them up and drop them as the horses pass the post. What would there be for the people who clear up the tracks to do, if we didn't? Anyway, that's why I'm hoping to be paid out for a winner who then loses the race.

Jackpot and Placepot

Considering the amount of effort which goes into the attempted solution of Tote Jackpots and Placepots, most punters are remarkably unsuccessful. I feel that syndicates are the answer to the former, as in each race there is only a single winner, whereas a careful individual can make a profit from the Placepot. Still, for the Jackpot, the fact that small-stake entries (ten pence minimum) can be placed at the track gives a chance on days when a banker bet or two can be found. Naturally luck plays as big a part as skill, not least in the fashion aspect of racing: a fancied horse ridden by a lesser jockey, as with Carroll at Ascot in 1993, will knock out many tickets.

The trick with Jackpots is to decide when to participate, for this is one of the rare instances in betting where you have numerically a better-than-level bet. Roulette gambling enables casinos to take a margin of 3 or 6 per cent, depending on whether there is a single zero or both single and double zero on the board; that is still far better than the odds against punters, with bookmakers framing their odds at between 15 and 20 per cent in their favour (the market permitting). But in the Jackpot, punters can be betting on much more favourable terms, even though the final payout is subject to a 30 per cent deduction by the operators. The reason is that as the pool develops, with non-winning days, it incorporates a growing amount of unclaimed money from earlier days. By way of explanation, here is a simple example of how it works.

After a few days, there can often be sums in excess of £100,000 being carried over. At that stage, there is usually around £80,000 (depending on the attractiveness and competitiveness of the meeting concerned) additional money, making a total of around £180,000. Should the Jackpot be won on that day, the £180,000 would be reduced by 30 per cent to £127,500, which means that each single pound of new money is worth a net 127,500 divided by 80,000, or just over £1.50. Attractive indeed. The only snag is getting the six winners; but you see what I mean in mathematical terms, I'm sure.

Once the pool does climb high, it seems to me there's little point in shooting for the lot, as one-pound lines are vastly too expensive. When pools reach several hundred thousand pounds, it's often better to restrict the unit stake to ten pence, to increase potential cover for the same stake. What's wrong with winning £20,000 from a declared dividend of £200,000? In such cases, if you were a sole winner, you'd have plenty of fire power to go for the even bigger pool the following day.

Over the years, the Tote Jackpot has had a chequered existence. In the 1960s very large pools occasionally accrued following several days when no racegoer had managed to select the necessary six consecutive winners. These large pools were very rare, depending almost entirely on big meetings such as Royal Ascot, Goodwood or Cheltenham to attract additional money over a period. For a while a five-race Jackpot was adopted, but this proved rather too easy for multiple operators to win, and the dividends were rarely large.

Now, though, the Jackpot has become the jewel in the Tote's crown. Since the inception of an arrangement with Corals, one of the big three bookmaking firms, to begin Tote Direct, a system where off-course money in Corals shops swells whichever of the Tote's pools the punter wishes to participate in, these Jackpot pools have grown much more rapidly. Racing may view the National Lottery with misgivings, but it will not be long before million-pound pools become commonplace in the Tote Jackpot, especially as Hills and Ladbrokes, the other two major betting chains, are carefully monitoring developments. Bookmakers who inject bets into Tote pools receive handsome commission rates.

Needless to say, winning the Jackpot takes plenty of luck and usually it is the multiple perm entries by major syndicate backers which have the best chance. Occasionally, though, a single line does come home for its jubilant winner.

Less ambitious betters are on much safer ground attempting to win the Tote Placepot. In this case, the punter need only find a horse to finish placed in each of the first six races on any programme, and dividends can be surprisingly high. It often takes just a single unplaced favourite to magnify a dividend many times over, and dividends of even £1,000 are not rare. Often, those of us who might have been tempted look back and say 'I'd have got that.'

Again, Placepot pools have been dramatically bolstered by

the effect of Tote Direct arrangements in Corals and other smaller multiples' shops. A bald comparison between total pools in 1993 and the corresponding days in 1994 indicated at least two or even three times the interest. At small meetings, which would have had minimal input on course, the pool can grow to even six or seven times the former level, and larger dividends are obviously possible. During the winter season of 1993–4, on those days when only a single meeting (usually on the all-weather) survived the elements, some pools reached almost £20,000; in the old days you'd have been lucky with an on-course pool of around £200.

With Placepot pools my preferred strategy is to go for a higher stake than the single pound and aim at one horse in each race, rather than attack with a perm. So often with a multiple entry, you find the fancied horses in each race all make the places and dividends can be very disappointing, often way below the eventually permed stake.

A variation, if you insist on more than one chance in each race, would be a 64-bet plan, with two runners in each race. But it's best in this case to take your first choice (presumably a fancied runner) and then couple it with a relative outsider. If one or two odds-on chances miss the frame, even on a day with few runners, dividends can be surprisingly high.

In small fields of two, three or four runners, it is necessary to find the winner. In these instances, I will take all of them, hoping for a shock, and have them with a single horse in the other races. A third favourite in a field of four is likely to appear on only about one-tenth of all Placepot entries for that meeting – ingredients for a big dividend.

Trio and Tricast

The Tote Trio is growing in popularity with racegoers, but if it is going to succeed, it needs to be seen to compete with the off-course bookmakers' Tricast. The difference, as with forecast bets (dual or either way on the Tote; straight, one-two in the correct order with bookmakers) is that in the case of the Trio, while the punter still has to find the first three home, the order does not matter. To that extent it is six times easier to get right than a Tricast as there are six ways in which any three horses can finish. Again, though, aiming at a Trio is only advisable where the pool is likely to be strong, that is, at the major meetings.

In the Tricast, there are certain times when the punter has value on his side, for instance when an apparent equality of chance for all the horses in a race is upset, usually by the draw advantage. Several tracks occasionally offer such a situation. Races like the 1994 Madagans Two Thousand Guineas, with the Newmarket track clearly favouring horses in the high numbers, or the Insulpak Victoria Cup at Ascot a few days earlier, when the high numbers also held an overwhelming advantage, cannot easily be predicted beforehand. Had it been possible to do so, a random bet on the three highest numbers in the Two Thousand Guineas draw (Mister Baileys, drawn 21; Grand Lodge, 22; and Colonel Collins, 23) would have yielded a big winning dividend.

More predictable is the effect of the draw on Sandown's five furlongs, especially in big fields on soft ground, when it pays to concentrate on the high numbers. Often, such minor factors as form can look meaningless compared with geography. I remember one day going to Sandown with the trainer Rod Simpson, who had a filly in a five-furlong nursery. She had only a place chance, and with the ground soft and a large field filling the stalls, I had the temerity to suggest that it would be a total waste of time to run straight up the track from that position. I reckoned his jockey would be better off allowing the rest to go and then crossing over to the far rail. As the field nears the finish there, horses often hang away from the rail as they tire, and while you'd need luck to get a run after forfeiting so much ground, it's still worth the risk.

After considering the idea, Rod discussed things with his jockey, who duly took the straight-down-the-middle course and finished tailed off last, almost a full furlong behind the winner. After a few strides out of the stalls, the field fanned out across the track, with the high numbers extending their advantage all the way to the line.

The Sandown Tricast was exploited with great skill two decades ago on the basis of the peculiarity of the five furlongs there by journalist Tony Hillier, who later emigrated to Australia. Patrick Cooper, a noted professional gambler, has also found Sandown a money-spinning track in such circumstances.

The sprint course at Thirsk can also provide similar chances, as the track bends slightly away to the right. A similar bend after the start affords a big advantage to high numbers in the draw at Beverley, but over recent seasons the number of winners coming wide has increased.

Pointers and pitfalls

The best way I can emphasize the following cautionary notes is to say that if I had only followed my own recommendations more often, I would be a happier and wealthier man and an altogether more convincing adviser.

To start with a 'don't': *never* bet odds on. For some reason, the British gambler (and he has his counterpart in every other country where racing takes place) nurtures the fond belief that if a horse is favourite it is likely to win. What he should think is that while on a random survey of a group of horses, *individually* it has less chance of losing than each of the others, *generally* there is more chance of its losing than winning.

At the course, the temptation to bet on odds-on chances is strengthened because there is no tax element. A hundred pounds to win eighty on a 5–4 on chance may not seem a terribly stupid thing to do, *until you try it*. You'll be shocked how often they do lose. Even worse is the same wager in a betting shop. There you'd either have to pay £10 extra for tax paid on, and receive just £180 (a profit of only £70 on £110 or 11–7 on) or merely accept £18 less return on a straight no-tax bet – in which case you'd win just £62 for your £100 investment: barely 5–3 on.

Even if you know your horse is a moral certainty, odds-on betting can provide a salutary, painful lesson. In late May 1994, at the picturesque Cartmel track, Peter Niven rode a 7–1 on chance against three no-hopers in a novice hurdle. Surrey Dancer, a winner three times and placed in his other two starts over hurdles, had also won and finished third in three recent Flat races. The almost certain runner-up, who started 7–1 against, was Rully, a bad selling plater on the Flat, around three stone (perhaps thirty lengths or a hundred yards) inferior to Mary Reveley's horse, and with a best hurdles performance of fifth last time out in a novice selling hurdle. Rully set off ahead around this sharp Cumbrian circuit, and although Surrey Dancer kept in close enough touch he never closed right up. At the finish Rully was drawing away again.

Examine what would have happened to a £700 bet on the course. The punter would have backed Surrey Dancer to win £100 and lost £700. Off-course, the same punter would have staked either £700 plus £70 tax to win £100 for a net potential profit of £30, reflecting actual odds of 30–770 – less than 1–25. If he did not pay tax on, he would have bet £700 to win £100 and be liable to £80 tax on the return, offering him true odds of 1–35.

There's no such thing as a certainty in racing. My view is that to risk more than you can win is stupid. Off-course, it's almost heresy.

*

On a more positive note: fix your stake, and be selective. If I'd been able to follow the first of those two principles I'm sure my own betting would have been much more profitable. The only sensible course of action is to begin with a bank, divide the bank into so many equal portions and proceed on a level-stakes basis. This will obviously deal with the times when you will strike long losing runs, and enable you to stay in with a shout until the end of that sequence of bets.

Being selective is also advisable, whether your preference is to bet in conditions races, where the weights are laid down according to the previous performances of the participants, to focus on two-year-old races, where form tends to be reliable (with the danger of high-class newcomers to racing altering calculations), or to specialize in handicaps. There is so much action now, so many betting opportunities, that if you spread your attention too thinly, natural erosion – and the fact that bookmakers do have a mathematical advantage over a series of races – will ensure you lose.

Within one's area of speciality, though, there sometimes comes an opportunity which all the instincts of the gambler will attempt to dissuade you from accepting. This is the time when you will be looking at a race, fearing your fancy will be at odds too restricted to back, only to find it may actually be offered as high as 3–1 or 4–1 against. The first instinct, of course, is to conclude that *it can't win*. The stable or the bookmakers must know something. Perhaps they do; perhaps the horse will trail home last and the odds will be correct. But in such cases, the *value* concept comes into play; and here, too, the usual rule for level stakes betting can be suspended. *Double the stakes*. That's my advice. If the horse loses, you've lost two of your units. My own feeling is that a total bank of thirty points (betting perhaps at £10 per point, depending on one's resources) is about right. So two losing points would not be terminally regrettable. I assure you, erring that way is preferable to allowing the horse to win without carrying any of your money.

This situation, clearly, can occur in reverse, and is a particularly dangerous one for the betting shop punter. Suppose you have made a selection, based on all the various aspects – form, going, distance, jockey, stable in form, track and so on – expecting a 10–1 chance. The opening show has the horse at 4–1 and its price continues to contract. You may have fancied it strongly; perhaps you've even been waiting for it. But if your estimation of its chance was 10–1, it is only a reasonable bet at 4–1 or less. The advice here is *halve your stake*. Then, if the horse does win, you have the satisfaction of knowing your judgement was correct, and you still showed a profit on the deal; if it loses, you've minimized the loss. This horse could well start at longer odds and do better next time. Indeed, the fact that it failed (not to cast undue doubts on the integrity of racing professionals) may in some part be a function of the unexpectedly poor price.

To return to the question of value, the first rule must be: *never be afraid of winning too much*. Obviously, the alarm bells do ring if the expected 10–1 becomes an actual 25–1, but the fact is that there are rarely good reasons why a horse should have less chance of winning if there is little stable money for him. John McCririck, whose energetic, individualistic performances as the betting expert on Channel Four Racing arouses critical and admiring comments in roughly equal measure, is a great advocate of the 'money talks' school of racing. If the market smells wrong about a horse he will say, 'This can't win.' Sometimes it doesn't; but other times it does, and always at much longer odds than expected.

*

These days, many more races have advertised morning prices with all the major high street bookmakers. It might seem an exceptional service for punters, but mostly it is an efficient way for the bookmakers to test the water early in the day, hours before the actual hostilities begin.

With their offices in places like Newmarket and Lambourn, Ladbrokes, above all the major firms, have a ready finger on the pulse of what is likely to happen, and their managers can soon tell, perhaps even from a bet as small as £10, when it comes from the right source in a particular stable, that a horse is expected to run well. How shrewd of them to spread the time-scale of betting to enable such calculations to be made, and odds to be altered accordingly.

I do not enjoy taking early prices, even when I'm fairly certain they will contract as the hours pass. Even worse, for me, is to open the racing papers to look at the *Racing Post*'s Pricewise column, or the *Sporting Life*'s Beat the Book feature, compiled by the youthful, aggressive Mark Winstanley, and find that one or both pinpoint a horse I've napped in my own paper that day. The inevitable result is a dramatic constriction in its odds; sometimes horses quoted at even 25-1 with a single out-of-step firm will end up at a quarter those odds at the start of the race.

One exception is on a Saturday when the big firms hold the prices until a certain time, allowing early shoppers to guarantee their odds. Another concession on some major races is the guarantee that if the starting price exceeds the early price taken, the punter is on at SP. The advice here, then, is *shop around*; but one warning. Concessions like these are most often available when the race is very difficult to unravel. They're not giving anything away out there.

CHAPTER THREE

A Great Day Out

IT IS EASY to be seduced by the warmth of summer; by blossom on the trees as Flat racing gathers momentum and by hot days at Royal Ascot when many of the best horses in the kingdom compete with a few invaders from France and Ireland.

It is also easy to forget, during those exciting days which seem to build week by week to the next climactic event, that the bulk of summer racing encompasses barely half of the year. So the regular racegoer has at least as much unseasonable weather to contend with; and as I've grown older, the summer's appeal has heightened while elements of the winter are less attractive.

One drawback to winter racing is the uncertainty as to whether a meeting will go ahead at all. For a racing writer trying to tip winners during the winter season, such uncertainty can be most infuriating. You could be on a roll, your main fancy is denied a run and the horse you would have made your nap selection duly wins at rewarding odds at another track luckier with the weather.

It is during those spells of climatic uncertainty that the all-weather tracks at Lingfield Park, Southwell and the latest addition, Wolverhampton, should theoretically come into their own, but there have been aspects of the first few years' activity at Lingfield and Southwell that have caused misgivings (more on this in Chapter 6). Still, all-weather action is here to stay, adding another strand to the kaleidoscopic pattern of British racing.

Courses: the best and the rest

Apart from France, where it seems almost every other town boasts a racecourse (many of which, however, stage perhaps a single meeting each year), the variety of Britain's courses cannot be matched anywhere in the world. The British climate provides the sort of turf which suits the hooves of horses, cushioning the impact which half a ton of horseflesh inevitably causes on the delicate legs that carry it, especially during jump races.

Some tracks in Britain are specialist Flat only or National Hunt only, but most double up with jumping in the winter and Flat racing during the summer months. They may be right-handed or left-handed; small circuits of little more than a mile or great galloping tracks of almost twice that distance. They cater for animals of varying abilities, from the top-class tracks like Newmarket and Ascot to the humbler 'gaffs' like Folkestone or Sedgefield.

Strangely, attendance figures tend not strictly to follow the quality of the sport on offer, except in obvious cases such as Royal Ascot, Cheltenham or the Grand National meeting at Liverpool. Perhaps it's not so strange, for my own interest is just as likely to be satisfied on a quiet, ill-attended Monday afternoon at Nottingham as on a prestige day at Sandown or Newbury. There is nothing more satisfying than to see a horse show promise before it has been recognized publicly, and that can happen at the lowliest as well as the swankiest racecourse.

One difference between the top and bottom strata is the standard and availability of facilities. Over recent years, several of the major tracks have rebuilt once inadequate grandstands – not always, it must be said, to the general approval of the public. Epsom's architecturally acclaimed Queen's Stand offers a brilliant landmark for miles around, but internally it has not pleased everyone with the accommodation offered. Smart restaurants and private boxes with superb views of that most scenic of downland turf tracks are fine – the cynics say – for those lucky enough to be able to afford or be invited to them, but other racegoers, even in the most expensive Members' enclosure, suffer by comparison. My own view is that it's a big improvement on what was there before and, like many other innovations, helps provide income on non-racing days from activities like conferences and business conventions.

Newbury's latest addition, the Berkshire Stand, has also been criticized for not allowing enough space for Members who are neither in a box nor in the excellent restaurant. But the critics seem to have forgotten just how little room there was in the old wooden stand that it has replaced. And, as at the rejuvenated Epsom, the Berkshire Stand is very pleasing to the eye as you approach the course. Newbury's enlightened management team, headed by Lord Carnarvon, the course chairman who is also the Queen's racing manager, are committed to further developments.

Lord Carnarvon is on record as saying he wants to see a

maximum daily entry charge of no more than five pounds. As it becomes increasingly important to cater for family days out, pricing will be crucial, with perhaps an entire family entering for the cost of one and a half adults.

Funding the fun

Yet despite the unparalleled variety and increasing comfort of Britain's racecourses, racegoing here, as a habit or as a pastime, has been in gradual decline ever since the postwar boom years. The main problem is the structure of financing British racing.

The two places in the world where massive crowds attend the track – Japan and Hong Kong – just happen to be two of the places where there is a Tote monopoly. In those Far Eastern environments, the rake-off for the sport from the massive betting aggregated ensures very strong prize money, excellent facilities and cheap admission. A major day's racing in Japan costs the racegoer less than fifty pence and he has around fourteen races to watch. Betting can be made by automatic machines which then dispense winnings. The long session is split, with an hour for lunch. Is there any wonder crowds approach 200,000 for the major events?

Here, betting revenues take much longer to filter down to racing. Racetracks do receive help from the levy on bets, and the Racecourse Association has also benefited from money generated by Satellite Information Services (SIS), which provides pictures of each day's racing and transmits the action to betting shops. But the tracks still rely for most of their revenue on admission charges to racegoers, and Britain (along with Ireland) – despite the best efforts of Lord

Carnarvon and others – is easily the most expensive among major racing countries, with a day in the Members' enclosure at the Cheltenham Festival costing £50.

But Britain and Ireland do have one thing which makes a trip to the races a uniquely pleasurable experience: namely, the line of bookmakers who shout the odds before every race and lend a characteristic atmosphere to the track. In France, the United States, Japan and Hong Kong there is no alternative to the faceless machine.

The choice seems clear: tradition and a pleasing on-course spectacle in Britain, with the consequent drawback that bookmakers and the state (by way of betting duty) devour the majority of betting money long before anything filters down to the people who put on the show; or, in other countries, a much duller experience, but at least with the knowledge that prize money and facilities can be fully catered for.

My own view is that if the British government had modelled the two varieties of on- and off-course betting on the Australian system, racing itself would have been much stronger than it is now and government revenue would still have been higher than is the case. Australian racing combines an off-course Tote monopoly with an on-course choice between track bookmakers and Tote betting. Strangely, far from weakening the on-course market, the reverse seems to be the case: Australian racing features many bigger betters than the British sport. Indeed, the view of many British racing professionals on the betting side is that the on-course market is terminally ill, debilitated by small attendances and the actions of the major betting firms.

Whichever system one prefers, there can be little doubt that a visit to the track is generally immeasurably more interesting than a few hours in a betting shop. For a start there are the horses; and there are the people – the chance to see a famous face among the jockeys, perhaps a personality from another sphere and, of course, the chance, when standing quietly at Ascot or Newbury racecourse, of suddenly finding the Queen walking past a few yards away. The Royal Family's difficulties over recent years have been well enough chronicled elsewhere, but come June at Royal Ascot, the crowds still throng to the Berkshire course in the hope of a glimpse of the monarch's outfit and the majesty of the drive down the course each day of the Royal Procession.

A guest at the races

Having helped organize a popular race series for the past two years for the Harcros Building and Timber Company, I have been lucky enough to see just how entertaining a day at the races can be for people with limited racing experience. Commercial firms have found that sponsoring races which identify their product or services and enable customers to enjoy their hospitality with lunch, tea and a fine vantage point from which to watch the sport is exceptionally good value. And the customers, in a different, more relaxed environment, are just as likely to increase their next order while the afterglow of a happy afternoon or evening remains in the memory.

Always, we advise the guests to take advantage of everything the course offers, urging newcomers especially to go and see the horses in the paddock; walk around the enclosures; look at the way the horses are prepared; and watch them coming back when the race is over to see how they look after their exertions.

Often the sponsors rent a box or dining room for the day, usually with a view either over the course or down on to the paddock. In either case, they tend to be close to the Tote facilities, and the inexperienced racegoer is usually best served by betting on the Tote, particularly if he or she is a small-stakes punter.

While the Tote on-course does not have quite the range of bets that it offers off-course, the range is still considerably wider in scope than that generally available from on-course bookmakers. In their case the only option is usually a flat bet on an individual horse, and many on-course bookmakers not only have quite large minimum stakes – some as high as £10 – but may also decline to lay each-way (win and place) wagers. The Tote bets each way in all races of five runners or more and also offers a dual (either way) forecast in which the punter must pick the first two horses in a race, as well as other more exotic bets (as the Americans would say). Another benefit of Tote betting is the rapidity of pay-out. At major meetings the queues can be lengthy, but if a horse wins a race comfortably, the chances are the signal to pay out will be made within seconds of the finish.

Two other bets which tend to attract support from occasional racegoers, as well as the hardened regulars, are the Tote Jackpot and Tote Placepot, each of which is based on finding six horses, either (in the case of the Jackpot) winning their race, or (with the Placepot) finishing in the places. Both are discussed in more detail in the previous chapter.

Watching the horses

One of the real bonuses of actually going racing is being able to see, close up, in the minutes before the action, the animals on which your hopes and money might ride, and to assess their mental and physical shape.

The tempo at the track alters subtly as the seasons change. Winter means jump racing and weather cold enough not just to keep the humans covered up, but also to encourage stables to delay stripping their horses for action until the last minute. For that reason I always find it difficult to assess the condition of horses accurately before many jump races. Large winter rugs stay on and only a small portion of the anatomy is exposed, leaving calculations about fitness and how well the horse looks in its coat decidedly sketchy.

That is why the advent of spring and Flat racing is such a joy. Warm weather translates itself to gleaming coats on the horses; fitness can be assessed, while other factors such as possible temperamental worries can also be judged.

A day's jumping is probably going to be a different experience, not least because of the wider range in both ability and facilities which jumps trainers offer potential owners. In recent years, Martin Pipe has been by far the most effective trainer in terms of races won. His regular tallies in excess of 200 in each of five successive seasons have been the result of supreme organization and the development of the biggest jumping string in racing history. Fitness has been the prime factor in his success, as a cursory inspection of the paddock before a race in which he has a runner will usually confirm. Sometimes his horses can look very light, but still they are rarely beaten through lack of fitness.

Apart from obvious exceptions like the Cheltenham National Hunt Festival, Kempton's King George meeting and Newbury's Hennessy Cognac Gold Cup day, much winter racing is carried out in front of smallish crowds. But as soon as spring arrives, Flat race enthusiasts gather in swiftly growing anticipation of the Classic races, for within six weeks of the season's opening at Doncaster, the first two of the five Classics will have been run.

It always seems such a rush. Around the training centres the leading yards will have been working their horses seriously for only a few weeks, yet by the time of the Craven meeting, Newmarket's first of the year in mid-April, most of the Classic hopes will be primed for a run. Amazingly, by the end of April, the fields that assemble in the paddock for the first two Classics, the One Thousand Guineas for fillies and the Two Thousand Guineas for colts (fillies are also allowed to run, but rarely do) generally look what they are — the cream of the Classic generation.

Many of the contenders will have had a previous run in one of the trial races and an obvious task for the novice racegoer, especially those whose previous knowledge has derived from betting shops and televised racing, would be to compare the horses physically from race to race. The colts generally warm up in the Craven Stakes at Newmarket; the fillies often take in the Nell Gwyn Stakes, also at the Craven meeting, for their preparation. Not only can the running vary from trial to Classic, but in many years the going alters markedly too. The ability to discern which horses have improved in fitness and general well-being in the intervening two weeks or so can be the key to finding a good-priced winner on the big day.

It will be rare for a horse to be fully wound-up on trials

day. The horse which goes round the paddock on that day with a gleaming coat, well-muscled quarters (the area behind the saddle) and a firm ribcage will be the exception. Note down on your racecard which horses looked in good shape and, especially, which looked a little dull in their coats, slack in their muscles behind the saddle and rather overfed around the middle. If any of these horses either showed prominently until running out of puff, or stayed on strongly at the end of the race without quite winning, they could be the ones to concentrate on next time.

In some years it is all too easy to alight on the probable winner. In recent history, Zafonic, the 1993 winner of the Two Thousand Guineas, came to the race as the champion two-year-old of the previous year, looked physically in a different league from his adversaries – stronger, bigger, fitter – and duly romped home in course record time.

The basic paddock criteria for major races also apply in smaller events. All horses in each of the major stables are treated in a roughly similar way. Their exercise times within that stable are usually similar, although the occasional horse might need extra serious training to get him up to race-course fitness, while other, more delicate types may take very little work. The trainer also stamps his own requirements on his staff, so that when the horses get to the track, those from a particular yard will have a distinctive look. Some have their coats brushed in particular patterns; sometimes manes are plaited; and accessories like sheepskin nosebands, or Australian bridles, with the orange rubber strip running down the horse's face, also help identify specific stables' runners.

It is also helpful, if you are fortunate enough to be able to pay regular racecourse visits, to compare the prototype look of horses from different stables. If the usual look is very hard-trained with little excess flesh and a horse arrives from that stable looking much bigger, that might indicate an interrupted training schedule. Similarly, a dry-looking coat on a horse from a stable whose runners are normally blooming could preface a poor run. I saw the former Champion Hurdler Granville Again before his first run for Len Lungo's Scottish stable in April 1994. His coat was dry and patchy and looked almost as though sawdust had been rubbed on it in places. He had been disappointing all season before switching from Martin Pipe, and his subsequent run at Ayr in the Scottish Champion Hurdle confirmed pre-race fears, even though he was sent off at only 3–1.

For every racegoer who has to have a bet in each race, there is the more cautious type who prefers to play the waiting game. In such cases, regular paddock inspections, as well as helping make a day at the races a very busy event, will soon give the racegoer a better understanding of horses as physical specimens.

Vantage points

The best place to see a race need not be the closest to the action. For example, at Ascot the top floor of the Members' stand gives an astonishing panoramic view of the whole circuit. From here, even the most competitive races – the Royal Hunt Cup at the Royal meeting in June often has a field of thirty-two runners – are relatively easy to interpret and follow. With television monitors to help you sort out the early stages of the races, if you are only trying to follow a few colours, especially those of the horse you fancy or have backed, this vantage point cannot be bettered.

Newbury's new Berkshire Stand and the Queen's Stand at Epsom also offer excellent viewing. Sandown's stands, while not rising as high above ground as those at Epsom, Newbury and Ascot, still offer exceptional race-reading conditions, as the track is a natural amphitheatre with all the action happening below the stands. Sandown is also an excellent place at which to watch from the grass verge just beyond the winning line. Many Sandown regulars forsake the main stand to watch from here.

The way in which stands are aligned has a lot to do with how satisfactory they are for racegoers. Many years ago I remember attempting to read races from the old press box at the now long defunct Alexandra Park course in north London, which was just a few miles from my home. 'Ally Pally' had its charms for me, not least that it had been possible sometimes to go there after football matches at the school playing field in Muswell Hill, but viewing was not one of them. For races run over a mile and one mile five furlongs, the horses would start in front of the stands, set off down the straight in the direction of Wood Green and go either once or twice round the 'frying-pan', which enclosed a cricket pitch, before flying back towards the winning line. From the stands much of the action was either out of view as they went round the frying-pan, or hard to interpret as the horses were going directly away from or coming straight at you. You would hang out from any secure piece of masonry to get a glimpse of the races. There were no closed-circuit televisions to follow the pattern of the race in those days, and even the commentators found Ally Pally difficult.

In 1993, the management team at Alexandra Park revealed that there was a chance of staging trotting meetings there, and I went down with the chief executive to view what remained of the old track. Some of the hard standing under the former stands remains, and much of the old turf can still be discerned, but nearly thirty years on the biggest surprise is just how narrow the small loop of the frying-pan was. Considering the speed at which they shot round it, the hard ground on which they often raced there at the regular evening meetings and the narrowness of the track, it's surprising there weren't more accidents.

When Alexandra Park closed in 1970, Windsor supplanted it as the Londoners' night-time track for summer racing. Windsor stages many evening meetings during the warmer months, and the track's proximity to central London (although it is further away than Ally Pally) and the late starting times ensure healthy attendances, especially if the sun has been shining during the afternoon.

Those sunny evenings do have one drawback. While it is always pleasant to stroll around the verdant areas behind the stands, race viewing becomes a difficult job, at times even a nightmare. Early in my Fleet Street career, I was sent to Windsor by the Press Association, whose racing desk produced a stream of renowned racing journalists, of whom Peter O'Sullevan, the late Peter Scott, Tony Morris and Jonathan Powell are among the best known, to do the race descriptions job. Those of us on the desk in Fleet Street occasionally took over when the regular course men were on holiday, and on this occasion Dai Davies and Norman Fairchild, the top team, had obviously taken a day out, possibly getting fitted for their morning suits for Royal Ascot.

My co-stand-in on that memorable evening was the late Peter Goodall, a great friend, whom I had first encountered when I was working on the *Greyhound Express* (old boys:

Harry Carpenter, Oliver Reed). Peter had been the PRO to the Greyhound Racing Association before joining the PA and he continued doing a gossip column for the soon-to-close greyhound daily paper. He would never claim to be a horse-racing expert, but his infectious enthusiasm invariably persuaded even the most reticent of interviewees to reveal an interesting fact to enliven the stories the PA sent out to all the national and local newspapers on its wire service.

Windsor offered particular problems for the descriptions man in those days. Official results by the judge ended at the fourth horse and although the *Sporting Life* had a regular helper who specialized in taking the 'runners-up', even he was not infallible; moreover, at the time he was technically in opposition, as our comments in running appeared in a rival publication.

Peter warned me of the difficulties, and as I awaited the start of the opening race, the Blue Charm Maiden Plate, a five-furlong maiden race for two-year-old fillies, I could hardly be said to be full of confidence. He said he would let the first four go and then give me the runners-up. 'We'll try for ten, but the first eight will do,' he said, as I glanced at the racecard, attempting to remember one or two of the twenty-six different sets of colours and wondering what I was doing there.

The sun shone brightly, quite low in the sky, almost directly behind the horses. My two memories of the race are clear. The favourite Boscage, trained by Bruce Hobbs, duly came away from her field, but the next bunch were quite close together. The Windsor press box is no more than 15–20 feet above ground and with the horses coming almost straight at you and the stands close to the track, it is not an easy job even for well-schooled professionals, which we were not.

I waited, pen poised over racecard, for Peter's salvation by numbers. He called out three, staccato-like, decisive, then added, lamely: 'missed them'. Waiting for the official verdict was not entirely pleasant, and when it was called Peter's first and second numbers corresponded to the third and fourth horses home. So we had the fifth, managed to drag the next three from the *Life*'s retainer, and spent the rest of the evening in trepidation.

They say that experience is the best remedy for ignorance. But for the rest of that year I had to live down my comments on another race, in which Eddie Reavey's sprinter Compensation Year figured in a tight photo-finish. I remember thinking the strong finisher had got the race, and my comments in the relevant form book indicated thus. The official form book, published by Raceform, had the real version of the facts, with the winner just defying the runner-up's late burst.

Just like at Ally Pally, the Windsor stands are poorly aligned. The track is a figure-of-eight, and there is an intersection a couple of furlongs from the finish. Viewing is reasonable when the horses are side-on, but during the crucial closing stages the horses are coming straight towards you. No wonder many racegoers stay in the bars to watch races there.

If you're on foot on the ground, of course, it's up to you how you align yourself, and for National Hunt enthusiasts there is no more intimate feeling at a race meeting than to go out into the centre of the track and watch the horses close to a fence.

At my grammar school in the City of London, our economics master must have been not only a racing nut but also a great sport, for I recall a day when we let slip we

56

had decided to cut someone else's dull lesson (British Constitution, I think) for a trip to Sandown Park. Upper-sixth privileges transcended A-level revision, no doubt, but it seemed the height of daring to us at the time. So, armed with one or two commissions for the economics master (don't worry: I ended up with a grade A – surely encouragement for the *laissez-faire* school of study), we took the train from Waterloo to Esher.

The ability to remember far-off events with great clarity must have something to do with the impressionability of youth. The day in question I can recall vividly. Flash Bulb, trained by Frank Cundell, and Wilmington, trained by Peter Cazalet, were fighting out the argument as they came to the Pond fence, where we had taken up our pitch. There was an exact division of opinion among us – two for Flash Bulb, two (my good friend Harry Hillier and I) for Wilmington, who won and looked sure to do so as he passed us. I can still see Bill Rees (on the winner) and Johnnie Haine coming to the fence, their faces revealing the combination of elation and trepidation which must be part of every jump rider's mentality as he goes out on each mount.

I often like to go out to the middle at Fontwell, where the odd hump enables you to get a good sight of the horses as they go around that tricky figure-of-eight. The alignment of the stands here is better than at Windsor, and racing incomparably more exciting.

Much less intimate is the middle of the track at Newbury. However busy the day there, the track is so vast that the sound from the stands, even as the horses approach the finishing line, is strangely muted. As for Ascot, there is little point in going into the middle. If you look carefully from the stands towards the point seven furlongs from home on the round course, you can make out a white sightscreen, which indicates the location of Royal Ascot Cricket Club. Each year the racing photographers play a match during the Royal meeting, and I have been a regular guest over the past few years. Standing in the centre of the pitch, you can see a small part of the course; but so vast is Ascot that a full-sized cricket pitch is only a tiny portion of the field, which also boasts a golf course (suspended during the Royal meeting, of course) and parking for thousands of cars.

As I said at the start of this chapter, the variety of race-course experience in Britain can be rich indeed. Taste it, smell it, feel it. The texture may change with the seasons, but the overall effect can be strangely intoxicating.

CHAPTER FOUR

A Year Round the Tracks

IN THE COURSE of a year I probably go racing between 200 and 225 times – and though it might sound embarrassingly uncritical, there is hardly a track which I do not anticipate visiting with pleasure, whether I am going as an integral part of a day's work or on an incidental whim.

Each one of Britain's fifty-nine racecourses has an individual feel. They differ widely, but it is just as easy to be fulfilled by an afternoon at Southwell, with its humble contestants, small crowd and feeble betting market, as the more obvious delights of the Rowley Mile at Newmarket in Guineas week. The tempo, naturally, differs, but the energy and interest which the locals display at Southwell as they try to unravel the mysteries of form, jockeyship, trainers' expertise and race distances, are just as much in evidence as at Headquarters.

So is the emotional roller-coaster of anticipation and (sometimes) achievement. It was at Southwell, in November 1993, that I was able to celebrate a narrow victory in the *Sporting Life* naps championship. My last nap of the season, Pharaoh's Dancer, was running in the final race of the day there. The only feasible opposition, the *Racing and Football Outlook*, had selected a horse in an early race at Folkestone. It seemed much more appropriate to travel up to Nottinghamshire from home to root for my choice rather than get to Folkestone and watch the rival's horse streak home. From Southwell I watched on the monitor as, after looking dangerous for a while, the would-be party pooper faded away, leaving me feeling curiously numb at the thought of a second win in the championship.

The thrill of competition through an eight-month season had been sufficient to keep the adrenalin coursing through the veins, and encourage concentration until the final day. Success, perversely, left an emptiness – but it lasted for no longer than it took me to order a couple of bottles for the boys in the Southwell press room.

*

I can't claim to have been to every single track in the land, and there are courses that have missed my company for twenty years or more: but it seems to me that as good a way as any to convey the kaleidoscopic variety of British racing is to follow the path I might take round the tracks as the year unfolds.

January

As long as the celebrations of the night before do not preclude an early start on the deserted roads, the racing year begins with New Year's Day at Cheltenham. With the days at their shortest, the elements are always dangerous, and a sharp frost is an ever-present threat. Among memorable

New Year's Days for me was the time in 1986 when my red colours (white spots on cap) were carried to success in the Steel Plate Trial Hurdle there by Tangognat, ridden by Peter Scudamore and trained by Rod Simpson.

Tangognat, by Dance in Time out of Aracara, was, I thought, quite neatly named. His dam's name was a palindrome, so I sought a palindromic name for him and luckily found, by experimenting with names of dances, one which did not sound entirely absurd.

The horse, a real star in the mud, had won twice within a few days by wide margins on the Flat at Kempton, and was destined to win twice at Cheltenham that January. He thus became one of the leading fancies for the Triumph Hurdle and Scudamore, who had ridden him in both those previous Cheltenham wins, was keen to ride him again.

The ground had been firming up for a few weeks, though, and David Nicholson, for whom Scudamore was then stable jockey, quite rightly invoked his claim on him. Solar Cloud, the Nicholson runner, was a 40–1 chance and regarded as a no-hoper, not least by his jockey. Nicholson, up to that time, had never won a race as a trainer at the Cheltenham Festival, and neither had Scudamore. Solar Cloud ended both ducks and was coming back to unsaddle by the time Tangognat limped home a long way back. The old boy was destined to race only once more (unsuccessfully) a year later.

It might not be much of a claim to fame, but on the only two occasions on which Scudamore sported the Stafford silks on a racecourse, he won prestige races at Cheltenham.

Beating the weather

Other January highlights include a very strong jumps programme in the middle of the month at Warwick. This
sprawling midlands track has retained many of its old
Victorian stands, to which has been added a functional and
rather faceless structure close to the paddock and weighing
room which provides boxes for sponsors and other commercial racegoers. This hotchpotch of buildings is spread out
along the length of the straight. A large hill in front of the
winning-post portion of the stands obscures much of the
action, but once the horses emerge from behind it with
around a mile to race, the action is hectic indeed.

The mid-January fixture offers several valuable races, some
of which often have a bearing on later events at the
Cheltenham Festival. Warwick often survives bad weather,
as in 1994 when the loss of Ascot the same day led to the
first instance of a race-day switch of a major event. The
Victor Chandler Chase was diverted from Ascot to Warwick
and was the forerunner of a similar relocation of the
Greenalls Gold Cup from abandoned Haydock to Kempton
the following month.

As well as their February clash, Haydock Park and
Kempton Park also coincide with their late-January jumps
meetings. Tracks which race on Saturdays during the winter
tend to offer excellent prize money, and both Haydock and
Kempton are utterly fair tracks where good horses should
have every chance if good enough. For this day I usually go
north to Haydock, and it was there in January 1994 that
Flakey Dove gave the first intimation, when winning the
Haydock Park Champion Trial, that she might indeed
develop into a Champion Hurdle contender seven weeks later.

Throughout the month it is impossible to evade the feeling that all the racing is leading up to something more important. Cheltenham is now less than six weeks away, and the fixture there at the end of January is another highly significant one. But also during those short, nippy days, the less glamorous tracks like Leicester, Nottingham and Southwell in the midlands and Lingfield and Fontwell in the south are worth a visit – pleasant ports of call, if a little spartan in appearance. The racing may not be brilliant, but the shellfish stalls are an attraction in themselves, with prawn curry both a worthwhile diversion and welcome insulation on a cold afternoon. Leicester has made minor improvements over the years; Nottingham has been slightly more adventurous, and has been rewarded by several competitive winter days.

Over the water

When the weather turns hostile in England during January and February, the Irish often enjoy better luck with the elements. A favourite trip for me is the late January Sunday fixture at Leopardstown which features the AEG Europe Champion Hurdle and one or two other extremely significant races, over both hurdles and fences.

Leopardstown, just to the south of Dublin, stages excellent sport throughout the year. For example, could there have been a more significant two-year-old race anywhere in Europe in 1993 than the Heinz 57 Phoenix Stakes in which Turtle Island, fifteen-length winner of the following year's Irish Two Thousand Guineas, beat Las Meninas, the heroine of the 1994 One Thousand Guineas?

Part of the appeal of Irish racing is the facility with which their best trainers adapt to either code, Flat or National Hunt. The great Vincent O'Brien operates nowadays at a much more leisurely level than formerly, but even before his heroic Classic-winning days he had been the most rapacious collector of jumping's top prizes, winning three Grand Nationals and a string of major events at Cheltenham Festivals. His protégé Tommy Stack, rider of Red Rum in his final Grand National triumph, is also an astute practitioner under both codes, and gained his big reward when Las Meninas edged out subsequent Oaks and Irish Derby winner Balanchine in the One Thousand Guineas at Newmarket in April 1994.

Jim Bolger and Edward O'Grady also keep busy during the winter, but if there is a present-day master of all branches of his art in Ireland, it must be the many times champion trainer Dermot Weld.

At this time of year Dermot is just as likely to be setting up a major winner for his principal owner Michael Smurfit by running candidates for the Cheltenham Festival as preparing Classic potential on the Flat; or, as was the case in January 1994, collecting the Irish Champion Hurdle with a Festival hope, in this case Fortune and Fame.

The criticism of jockey Adrian Maguire – that he had 'gone too soon' on Fortune and Fame – was even adhered to by Weld himself. No doubt the later exploits of the novice Danoli, runner-up at Leopardstown, but an emphatic winner of the big stayers' novice hurdle at Cheltenham, and then also of Liverpool's Martell Aintree Hurdle, in which Fortune and Fame was third, put that criticism into perspective.

Weld, of course, had already earned fortune and fame for himself two months earlier, when Smurfit's best hurdler – he did not run over jumps during that winter – Vintage Crop proved his own and his trainer's versatility in full measure by beating the Australians in the 1993 Melbourne Cup.

Weld and stable jockey Michael Kinane, another consummate professional, had proved too tough for the antipodeans, who reckoned the fact that Vintage Crop had not raced for a month beforehand – their own horses not uncommonly run twice in the week leading up to the Cup – meant the invaders could not possibly hope to win the race. They did, and easily, earning both men and their horse great prestige.

That January card at Leopardstown also features a top juvenile hurdle, the Irish version of Cheltenham's Arkle Chase and also the Leopardstown Chase, nowadays a poor shadow of its earlier incarnation when first Arkle and then his stablemate Flyingbolt exerted such superiority over their contemporaries.

February

The screws tighten

The hunt for Cheltenham Festival clues is now all-pervading. Each ripple in the ante-post market on the Cheltenham Gold Cup, the Champion Hurdle and the Triumph Hurdle is given maximum publicity by the high-fliers among the press corps whose preoccupation with the thoughts of the bookmakers' PR men can be taken to absurd lengths. Mike Dillon of Ladbrokes is the doyen of the 'bookies' runners' and as the big days approach he is likely to be interviewed on television or quoted in the newspapers as often as many of the leading trainers with Cheltenham aspirations.

Dillon, confidant of many trainers, is also a Manchester

United fanatic, and the world champion in the acquisition of tickets to major events. His confidentiality and integrity are a byword in the industry and he is clearly the benevolent race-course face of Ladbrokes, whose acumen in the free-for-all of the racecourse betting market owes much to Dillon's knowledge.

Throughout February the clues come thick and fast. Early in the month at Sandown, races offer indications of potential Triumph Hurdle four-year-olds, Champion Hurdle types and novices aiming at the Arkle Chase at Cheltenham.

Ascot is not everyone's favourite course for watching jumpers – for a start, the horses are even further away on the jumps track than they are for Flat racing – but the early February fixture is always well contested and the Reynoldstown Chase, for novices over three miles, is a nice warm-up race for the three-mile Sun Alliance Chase at Cheltenham.

Even better Festival hints are offered by events at the end of the same week, when Newbury holds its Tote Gold Trophy meeting. This handicap hurdle was for many years sponsored by Schweppes, who gained lasting publicity from the many contentious issues thrown up by the race's early history. The late, great Ryan Price, attracted by the race's generous prize money, prepared his horses with military precision to arrive at the post in prime form, and they often showed marked improvement on earlier performances, incur-ring much official wrath.

Schweppes eventually gave up the race a few years ago, settling instead on a Flat race handicap at the Goodwood meeting in late July/early August, leaving the Newbury race to be picked up by the Tote. If some renewals of the Tote Gold Trophy have lacked the competitive nature and raw publicity appeal of the earlier Schweppes races, the 1994 version was a worthy echo of the early days. The first three home at Newbury were Large Action, Oh So Risky and Flakey Dove: a finishing order exactly reversed when the trio also filled the first three places in that year's Champion Hurdle just over a month later at Cheltenham.

Out into the country

Some of the smaller tracks stage their better meetings, weather permitting, in February. I always like to travel the hour or so north from Hertfordshire to Huntingdon's February fixture. This compact track offers a very fair running surface, fast-draining ground – and a fine view of the A1. The fences are well spaced and horses tend to jump them with comfort. High-class runners are rare, but the Sidney Banks Hurdle, over two and a half miles, often attracts a novice with Cheltenham intentions.

Nor is it just the major tracks which are targeted by the punters. Throughout the winter and early spring, Uttoxeter, near Stoke-on-Trent, pulls in good crowds in eloquent testimony to the marketing skills of Stan Clarke, its owner, who has transformed the course into a financial goldmine in a few short years. Facilities are good and the careful husbanding of the course has led to its attracting some high-class horses, especially novices starting out on their jumping careers.

Wincanton, like the other west country courses Newton Abbot and Exeter, has its hard core of regular patrons, and the car parks are inevitably full when I enter the gates, generally a few minutes before the start of the opening race. In the old days, the road down to Wincanton was one of the slower routes on the annual itinerary, but the A303 is now much improved. It is easy, then, to forget just how far away that part of the country is from the M25; but if you time your arrival for when most of the crowds are already installed, the last few miles generally offer a clear run. If you're thinking of going there, though, make an earlier start and give yourself time to work out your strategy for the day.

We still consider races like the Jim Ford Challenge Cup (Gold Cup) and the Kingwell Hurdle (Champion Hurdle) important Cheltenham trials, but in reality, the proliferation of such options elsewhere, usually for considerably more money, has tended to devalue them in that respect.

In praise of Kempton

The end of February is always a crucial time in my mind. Haydock, when it escapes the ravages of Lancashire's winters, and Kempton offer the final pieces in the Cheltenham puzzle. The second day at Kempton, always significant for the Racing Post Trophy, exceeded the claims of even its most fervent admirer – me – in 1994 when a string of Cheltenham Festival winners warmed up there.

Many believe Kempton to be a featureless track, offering an easy three miles and making less demand on stamina than on speed. But on soft ground, or with high-class horses in opposition, I believe it is one of the fairest stamina tests in the country. Let me offer a few instances, beginning with the single performance which, in all my experience of racing, has ever come close to matching the exploits of the great Arkle. Like Arkle, Captain Christy was trained in Ireland, coincidentally by Arkle's rider, the late Pat Taaffe, and had already won the 1974 Cheltenham Gold Cup when he turned up at Kempton for the King George VI Chase on Boxing Day the same year. Gerry Newman, an inexperienced young Irish rider, took the mount, and Captain Christy sailed off in front, jumped every fence with the greatest of accuracy and came home thirty lengths clear of the brilliant former Champion Hurdler Bula.

Later in his career, I was in Paris to see Captain Christy attempt a similar achievement in the Grand Steeple Chase at the Auteuil track. This was a significantly longer race and the French specialists all lined up to challenge as he again made the running. Captain Christy still led as the field came to the last of the obstacles but tired on the run-in, finishing a close third. Nevertheless, for a short time he was undoubtedly the top of the crop.

Twenty years after Captain Christy's King George, in February 1994, the going at Kempton was soft and the fields were top-class. Balasani, who won the Rendlesham Hurdle over three miles, went on to win the Bonusprint Stayers' Hurdle at Cheltenham; Arctic Kinsman, third in the Dovecote Novice Hurdle at Kempton, was a 50–1 winner of Cheltenham's Supreme Novice Hurdle the following month; Mysilv, successful in the Adonis Hurdle at Kempton, maintained her pre-eminence among four-year-olds by taking the Daily Express Triumph Hurdle at the Festival, while Pendil Novice Chase winner Monsieur Le Cure followed up in the Sun Alliance Chase at Cheltenham.

If even those successes don't prove my point, consider the Racing Post Trophy, quite rightly regarded as the supreme three-mile handicap chase of the whole season. Its 1994 winner Antonin won Cheltenham's Ritz Club Chase; The Fellow, third in the Racing Post Chase, collected a long-overdue Tote Cheltenham Gold Cup three weeks later; and finally Elfast and Fighting Words, fourth and sixth past the post at Kempton, also won races at the Festival.

That February Kempton meeting is also indelibly engraved on my heart for less happy reasons, associated with pursuit of the top slot in the *Sporting Life* naps table. For a number of years, I had my first real chance to test my tipping ability through the medium of the now defunct racing weekly, *The Racehorse*, published by Raceform, the small firm run by Ian de Wesselow which also produces the official form book. During the autumn of 1974 I took over from that excellent judge Jack Millan, who had left to start his highly successful time as Robin Goodfellow on the *Daily Mail*, as part-time editor of that magazine. Somehow I managed to fit two mornings in *The Racehorse*'s offices in Battersea, and a full day (my *Daily Telegraph* day off) at the printers on Wednesday, into a six-day week, including Saturday night sub-editing the football reports on the *Sunday Telegraph*.

Within a week or so of taking over, an amusing incident occurred. My front-page piece in the first issue of *The Racehorse* under my direction was on the Cesarewitch at Newmarket. I had latched on to a light weight, trained at Epsom and ridden by Tommy Carter. Ocean King, a 25–1 chance, duly won, helping to push *The Racehorse* up quite a few places in the *Sporting Chronicle* naps table, which ranked just over a hundred competing tipsters from various publications around the country. A few days later a letter arrived addressed to Roger Jackson, now the greyhound open race expert with the *Sporting Life*, but then working mainly for the de Wesselow family on their other, slightly more down-market weekly, the *Winner*. The letter was from Peter O'Sullevan, who, as later experience has shown, is always extremely supportive of young racing writers. He congratulated 'Roger' on tipping the winner of the Cesarewitch and wished him luck in his new job.

Years later I mentioned the letter to Peter, and often when I see him now, I remember it with an inward smile. I also told him about the day at Newbury when I should have been at home revising for the following day's A level economics exam, but instead found myself standing in the betting ring, having backed O'Sullevan's tip for a fillies' race, and seeing him back another horse, which duly romped home. For a while my faith in all tipsters, and Peter in particular, was clouded. Now, though, I occasionally stand up before a gathering of racegoers, going through my thoughts on a particular meeting, and cannot always remember what I've tipped in the morning paper that day.

Some years on during my *Racehorse* tenure, I felt sure that, after a couple of near misses, I could win the *Sporting Chronicle* table. For once, neither the highly astute Jeff Ross nor (to my mind) the greatest tipster of them all, Dick Adderley, who did the 'Beat the Book' feature in the *Chronicle* (he's now a betting synopsis reporter), was in touch as I held a forty-point lead coming to the late February meeting at Kempton. I thought that if there was going to be a worry it would come at Cheltenham, and I waited for a mundane novice chase at Kempton in the knowledge that my lead was safe.

Five minutes later, as the unfancied Balmers Combe came home under Mr Oliver Sherwood, I felt a niggle of recognition. 'Somebody gave that', I thought, and so he had. Teddy Davis of the *Chester Chronicle* had tipped Balmers Combe – and he had already been in the top six, about five pounds behind the second-placed man. I remember John Stubbs, the

71

Sporting Life's betting man, coming back to the press box and saying, 'The winner's 66–1.' I suggested that might be excessive and he said, 'We nearly made it 100–1, it was that in one place.'

Needless to say, there was no coming back from that sort of hammer-blow; but knowing Teddy, you could never begrudge him a win like that. He still turns up regularly at Chester and Haydock and we always enjoy a laugh about Balmers Combe. Of course, the horse never looked like winning another race, never mind one at Kempton.

March

Longer days, less frost and snow and some acceptable fare at Newbury and the Grand Military meeting at Sandown fill the time between the end of the trials and the arrival of the Festival.

At the Grand Military meeting, you are assailed at the entrances by soldiers collecting for military charities. Inside, the atmosphere is always upbeat and optimistic among race-goers, while the press room is almost totally obsessed by thoughts of Cheltenham a couple of days later. Several of the boys are already preparing to go down to Cheltenham on Sunday morning, to take up residence in their billets and to get an early sight of the action on the course gallops on Monday morning.

I prefer to delay the drive down until Tuesday morning, and invariably arrive in the press room to find the chairs all occupied and usually a newsroom colleague (or two) from the *Telegraph* perched in what would be my seat at any other meeting at the track throughout the year.

I'll come to aspects of the Festival elsewhere. For now, I will simply say that these three days provide a level of competition which by Thursday night has effectively brought the entire season to a climax. Even with almost eleven weeks of jumping left, for me it's just about time for Flat racing to commence – just as by Champion Stakes day in October I'm wishing they'd pack off the Flat horses until spring.

The start of the Flat

For as long as I can remember, the start of the Flat has been an exciting time in the rhythm of the sporting year. First at Lincoln, a track which sadly I never got to see, and since the 1960s at Doncaster, newspapers were united in telling their readers that the proper racing was back.

'They're off!' would be the back-page headline, and a photograph of the start of the first race of the year, with the horses spread right across the track, would accompany those hackneyed but immortal words.

The first race was always an apprentice event and perhaps twenty-five pale, skinny hopefuls would go down to the start and come back for a mile race on the Lincoln Handicap track. It always seemed to me that when the track management started messing about with this apprentice race, altering its position and distance and then totally removing it from the meeting, one strand was unnecessarily lost from the tapestry of the racing year. The picture of the proud young man with the caption 'Leading jockey – for half an hour' always caught the eye; but of course, the 'start of the Flat' no longer has that clear definition because of the proliferation of out-of-season all-weather activity.

The jockeys' title race has been either a victim or a beneficiary of the all-weather action, depending on your point of view.

For those regular protagonists in the title race, Pat Eddery, Michael Roberts and Willie Carson, it came as quite a shock when their return to action in March 1994 left them more than fifty wins adrift in the jockeys' championship behind the young Italian Lanfranco Dettori, who rode throughout the winter at Southwell and Lingfield, setting up a long lead over his perceived major rivals, with only the 1993 apprentice champion Jason Weaver managing to keep even remotely within reach.

The extra four and a bit months' racing on top of the traditional portion of the year must make it possible for records to be set, and Dettori had set a seasonal tally of 200 winners as a target early in the turf season.

Two hundred wins for a Flat jockey needs to be put into historical context. During the last century, Fred Archer, champion in thirteen consecutive seasons from 1874 to 1886, achieved a double century eight times, with 246 in 1885 his highest tally. Between 1886 and 1989 only one other jockey, Sir Gordon Richards, could equal that achievement. Like Archer, Richards' dominance over his contemporaries was total, and in a 28-year period, from 1925 to 1953, he was champion an astonishing twenty-six times. Also like Archer, his ability to 'fly' the starting gate in those days before the introduction of stalls contributed to his extraordinary success rate. On twelve occasions he exceeded 200 wins in a year, his 269 in 1947 never looking likely to be seriously challenged.

Now, with so much extra racing and planes or helicopters to take the jockeys to more than one meeting in a day, the opportunity is there for Richards' seemingly unassailable record to be eclipsed. But since his day, such brilliant champions as eleven-times winner Lester Piggott, the great

Australian Scobie Breasley, America's Steve Cauthen and Willie Carson have all failed to get to 200 in a calendar year. Pat Eddery (in 1990) and Michael Roberts (in 1992) did make the magic figure; Eddery's score of 209 and Roberts' of 206 were aided by regular use of private planes, limiting the fatigue which long hours on the road have always caused jockeys. With neither aircraft nor regular night racing to help him, the achievements of Richards are truly astounding.

The Lincoln

Until the advent of all-weather racing, the Lincoln was the sort of race which the bookmaking fraternity would anticipate with great relish. As the name suggests, it was formerly staged at Lincoln, with fields in the post-war period only once falling below thirty (twenty-nine in 1955, when Military Court won) and peaking to a highest-ever fifty-eight in 1948 when the eight-year-old Commissar came home in front. When the Carholme course closed after the 1964 season, the race moved to Doncaster with the rest of the opening fixture, Old Tom beating thirty-seven rivals to win the first Town Moor Lincoln. A year later there were forty-nine runners, of which Riot Act, trained by Sam Armstrong, took the honours.

Since the advent of stalls starts, a maximum of first twenty-six, then twenty-five and now twenty-four horses has been accommodated in the race; for horses that don't make the Lincoln proper, the sponsors have now added a substitute race in the Spring Mile, run the previous afternoon over the same course and distance.

When I suggested that until the start of the all-weather the

Lincoln was a bookies' dream, I was primarily referring to the fact that it came at the start of the year, when none of the horses had yet run; but also, and more crucially, it was run over a straight mile, which by its very nature presented the jockeys with the seemingly impossible decision as to which side of the track was the faster. It was thought, when the Spring Mile was introduced in 1993 for those horses which missed the main race, that a clue would be provided as to which side was preferable. It hasn't been that simple. In 1994, a seventeen-horse field in the Spring Mile raced home up the stands side, yet just twenty-four hours later all the Lincoln action was on the far side of the track.

There was a single year in which the experiment of running the race over the round mile at Doncaster was tried. Captain's Wings, the heavily backed favourite, duly won the race, and William Hill, the sponsors, were keen for the experiment to be discontinued. They got their wish.

One change to the race, of course, has been the chance for trainers to decide whether to adopt the traditional training schedule for a Lincoln candidate, or merely to jog along with races on the all-weather to get the horse fit and ready for the big day at Doncaster. In recent years, both camps have had their successes. Jimmy Fitzgerald and David Barron won with all-weather graduates Evichstar and Amenable in 1990 and 1991; since then, the old-fashioned approach has worked with High Low, High Premium and Our Rita.

Brighton on the rocks

It's years since I've been up to Catterick Bridge, but my memory is of a tidy little track where races are run at a true

76

pace. Their late March fixture might be only a low-grade affair, but, like its southern counterparts at Brighton and Folkestone during the same week, it reinforces the fact that the Flat is taking over.

Racing at Brighton is indelibly engraved on the mind, as much by Graham Greene's *Brighton Rock* and images of Richard Attenborough's menacing face as by the racetrack itself. I've always found it compelling, but one day when I had a runner there, it proved less than ideal. I had acquired very cheaply the one-time fair miler Fiefdom and sent it along to Rod Simpson to see if it could win a small race. For all his qualities as a horseman, Rod has a quirky attitude to certain aspects of his profession, not least to jockeys, and his preference for his own men, like Simon Whitworth and Dean Gallagher (both of whom ended up with him on my advice anyway), often paid dividends. But for this Brighton race, which was for apprentices with limited experience, I felt that someone with a few winners would give his mount a tremendous advantage. Early negotiations with the Luca Cumani stable established that one of the Italian trainer's young lads would be free to ride; but Rod insisted on his own apprentice, who rejoiced in the name of Frankie – sadly, not Dettori.

In the paddock we awaited the arrival of the jockeys. As Frankie approached I could hardly believe my eyes; facial hair on a jockey is an almost unheard-of phenomenon, and yet on that youthful visage – he was around twenty-one – there was a far-from-wispy moustache!

Rod and I had already discussed tactics, for Brighton can be difficult, especially from the mile starting gate. Frankie was to keep to the outside, as the ground was riding soft, and challenge up the stand rails.

Never have tactics been so minutely observed. As the rest of the field left the stalls, heading straight down the course, Frankie did a right turn, only failing to get to Haywards Heath because the outside perimeter rail was in the way. The field hurtled along, with Frankie and Fiefdom some way back, but in the last furlong, as the horses in the middle of the track began to tire, Fiefdom and his partner flew home, getting within a neck or so at the line. Fiefdom had started 10–1. You could say he was an unlucky loser, and a couple of subsequent wins, at Folkestone and Lingfield in the space of a week, would have backed you up. Later that year, Fiefdom was sold to my great friend, the County Durham sheep farmer Wilf Storey, who kept him going to the ripe old age of twelve, after which he became the property of Sharron Murgatroyd, the former jockey whose riding career was cut short by serious injury.

April

The pulse quickens

On the gallops around the country, the best of the previous year's juveniles are sharpening up for their pre-Classic tests. Easter beckons, and immediately thoughts turn to Kempton Park and one of the most unexpected incidents in my racing experience.

If you take a once-raced three-year-old, who had previously managed to finish third in a Leicester claiming race when he could have been collected for a mere £10,000, and take him to Kempton to oppose a field of choicely bred horses from the top stables, you might expect at best to finish in the pack. But at Kempton on Easter Monday 1985, when Tangognat, originally bought for just over £3,000 on the advice of Zara Pratt (now Zara Johnston, wife of blood-stock publisher John), lined up at 20–1 for the Ruth Wood maiden over a mile and a half, we did feel we were in with a bit of a chance, despite the fact that the field included the highly regarded Fire Of Life, trained by Ian Balding, and a $2.6 million horse trained for Khalid Abdullah by Guy Harwood. For the ground that year was bottomless early in the season, and Tangognat loved the mud.

Rod, undaunted by the moustachioed Frankie, had found another seven-pound claimer in Kenny Radcliffe, a Liverpudlian with (thankfully) rather more experience and considerably more idea than his predecessor. As the field turned for home, with three furlongs to go, we could see Kenny cutting the corner to challenge on the inside of his field. Almost unbelievably, Tangognat's bay head went to the front around the two-furlong pole, and within yards he'd streaked away, eventually coming home twenty lengths clear of Fire Of Life.

It was not until that horse collected the Italian St Leger later in the year that we were truly able to assess the enor-mity of Tangognat's victory. All the same, standing in the winner's enclosure, making the odd offhand remark to one's colleagues in the press, it was easy (too easy) to imagine one was Robert Sangster incarnate.

Perhaps we didn't believe it. There was another Kempton meeting later in the week, four days later to be exact, and we decided to let Tangognat take his chance. The ground remained soft, and the race was a furlong shorter, but Rod would not hear of defeat. Leaving the paddock before the race, I bumped into Clive Brittain, who was running a nice

Shirley Heights colt. 'Yours will need to be good to beat mine,' Clive said. He was right – we had a six-pound penalty; but it made no difference. Tangognat came home in front again (though only by fifteen lengths this time; clearly he was going backwards . . .).

Sad to say, the inevitable jump in class proved his undoing. He went next for the Chester Vase, in which he met Law Society and subsequent King George VI and Queen Elizabeth Diamond Stakes winner Petoski, as well as Miller's Mate, who broke a leg at the turn into the home straight. Tangognat's collapse was not quite so dramatic, but on ground turning faster by the hour after the effects of wind and sun, he came home a long way last of the four finishers and never raced on the Flat again. That's racing: elation followed by despair. For most owners, there's far more of the second type of experience than the first, but Tangognat had done me proud: those two wins at Kempton and two over hurdles at Cheltenham could not have been bettered.

Aintree

Between Easter and 'proper' Flat racing, there is the minor diversion of three days at Liverpool. Some years it's merely exciting. In 1993 it was just bewildering, with two false starts, the second of which was ignored by half the jockeys, and the 'race' having to be declared void. We'll come to Aintree, along with Cheltenham, Ascot and Goodwood, later on.

Home again

You may think I've despatched the three-day Aintree fixture with undue haste. In some ways, that's how I view it at the time. News of gallops at Newmarket in which Classic hopes are coming to the boil leaves one's thoughts if not one's body a couple of hundred miles to the south-east of that drab spot of real estate on Merseyside.

Not that the Rowley Mile in early April is always that much more welcoming. Some years, the east winds blow across the track with such biting ferocity that you'd believe you were where they started their journey west, back in deepest Siberia. As the locals in Newmarket never tire of telling you, 'They come straight here from Russia, there's nothing in between to stop them.'

In April, the horses often betray the elements. Unlike some racegoers, who believe that the false dawn of spring will be just as emphatic on the open spaces of the Newmarket Heath as in gentler, more protected regions of the south-east, the horses hold on to their winter garments, unwilling to expose themselves too early. Fillies, in particular, can look woolly, sad specimens; but by the next Newmarket meeting, they're gleaming with new-found health and confidence.

These are the crucial days. If you have a Classic prospect, time is short. Traditional training methods normally comprise two 'serious' working days each week, when the really strong work is usually asked of the horse, with cantering days and the odd easy day in between. Yielding to the temptation to overdo it in the early stages of the season can leave a horse needing weeks to recover rather than preparing it for its first race of the year. When strong work begins, there may be no more than three weeks before the first prep race for the Guineas; scope only for about half a dozen strong pieces of work. There's so little margin for error: running a horse before it's ready can be just as damaging as overdoing

81

the preparatory work. The winners of the two spring Classics have overcome many potential pitfalls along the way.

The wet spring of 1994 was particularly hostile for preparing horses, and strangely neither Mister Baileys, winner of the Two Thousand Guineas, nor the Irish filly Las Meninas, who collected the One Thousand, had been given a preparatory race. Those horses that did race previously encountered much faster conditions at the Guineas meeting than earlier that month, and perhaps suffered from the contrast.

Keeping the horses happy

Much has been written in recent years about what is perceived as a crucial change in training patterns, largely because of the startling success of one west country stable.

Miinnehoma's victory in the 1994 Martell Grand National crowned a long period of great numerical success for Martin Pipe without, it must be said, consistent harvesting of the top races. But in 1993 he won the Smurfit Champion Hurdle at Cheltenham with Granville Again and no doubt a Gold Cup will follow. What Pipe has achieved, in contrast to his adversaries, has been a tremendous tally of winners. Until the 1993–4 season, he had passed the 200 mark in five successive jumps campaigns; no other National Hunt trainer had ever even come near 200 winners in a single season. The methods behind such a record obviously call for serious evaluation.

Martin Pipe, son of a west country bookmaker, took out his first trainer's licence in 1977 and has since developed his Pond House stables at Nicholashayne, near Wellington in Somerset, into a high-tech showplace. The potential drawbacks of limited space for gallops have been mitigated by the introduction of other facilities, among which a swimming pool, a laboratory for testing various aspects of the horses' condition and, above all, a programme of repetitive 'interval' training aimed at producing horses at maximum fitness levels, are the most vital.

Pipe has also been astute enough to employ the best riding talent. His association with the recently retired former champion Peter Scudamore brought benefits to both men; now the reigning champion, Richard Dunwoody, has taken Scudamore's role as stable jockey and has gradually adapted to his altered situation.

Organizational ability, the sharpness of mind to seek out winning opportunities, notably for some of the lesser animals which have come into his care, and the skill to keep improving those animals have been Pipe's trademarks. It may still be too early to assess whether he is likely to maintain his progress to the extent that he will one day be able to challenge the top Flat-race trainers, but his increased activity on the Flat in 1994 suggests that he will be trying to make that breakthrough.

Pipe is not the only leading trainer to make light of restricted galloping facilities. Nigel Twiston-Davies, whose business partner Peter Scudamore is now also his assistant trainer, uses a short gallop up a hill to prepare his string for action, and the success of the novices Captain Dibble (1992) and the six-year-old Earth Summit (1994) in the Stakis Scottish Grand National show that stamina-building does not necessarily require long galloping exercise.

The remarkable Mary Reveley, who trains from her family farm at Saltburn, near Redcar, also makes do with a short gallop. Her success on the Flat as well as over jumps has been based on keeping her horses happy; and if there is a common theme among both the new school and adherents of the traditional methods still practised in Newmarket and Lambourn, it is the conviction that keeping the horses happy remains the most crucial factor.

Over the bridge to Beverley

While the big events continue to arrive with increasing frequency, April offers a number of lesser meetings with their own charm. One pleasant experience for me is to drive up to Beverley, one of my favourite northern tracks. The last few miles really lift the spirits, as the road passes across the dramatic span of the Humber Bridge and into the attractive east Yorkshire town with its Minster and, beside the track, a mile or so out of the town centre, the common land on which anyone is entitled to graze sheep under ancient by-laws. The turf on the course itself gleams on a sunny day, and the horses seem easily to cope with what may at first appear difficult gradients. Certainly the steep uphill finish makes it a decent test of stamina, and that's why I reckon it to be such a fair track.

I spend some time each week talking to the young Newmarket trainer David Loder about his horses. Having over twenty-five years come to know a number of trainers well, I have no hesitation in predicting a bright future for him, and he made a great start in his first full season in 1993 with forty-five domestic wins and one overseas winner. Quite early in our discussions I was suggesting several races at Beverley for his horses, and his strike rate there since has been most impressive. The track offers opportunities for horses just below top class and for him, as well as for me over the years, Beverley has proved a lucky course.

Back down south, Sandown stages a unique April meeting which once followed hard on a three-day spring fixture at Epsom. The loss of that meeting has left a gap in the southern early-season calendar, but at least the danger of a wet spring causing serious damage to the track before the Derby meeting is nowadays avoided. On the other hand, it seems to me a shame that we have lost some of the old Derby trials, and I think a number of them would be welcomed back if it were possible to revive them. Having said that, just why I can recall Hethersett beating River Chanter and Heron at Brighton one April, for instance, in a three-horse race for the long discontinued Derby Trial – distances three lengths, six lengths – is uncertain, except that Hethersett, the 1962 St Leger winner, was one of my favourite horses at the time my interest in racing germinated.

In those days, I belonged to a club in East London which was supported by Eton College. It was called Eton Manor and its facilities compared to those of other clubs were exceptional, considering that the fees were modest. I used to play cricket for this club, but once the racing bug had bitten deep, cricket matches were tricky affairs. Captaining a side, for instance on the occasion when Relko was due to attempt to follow his 1963 Epsom Derby success in the Irish Sweeps Derby, involved a delicate decision and careful timing. I'd just scored a quick fifty and managed to be run out just in time to race back to the clubhouse as the television showed the horses down at the start. In fact I was too punctual: if I'd known there would be a delay because of Relko's lameness, which caused his withdrawal – leaving the coast clear for Ragusa – perhaps I'd have stayed at the crease a little longer.

As my interest in racing and belief in my own judgement

increased, so my bored colleagues at Eton Manor coined a term of derision, not always received in the spirit it was intended. Captain Coe was the *nom de plume* of Tom Cosgrove, one of the tipsters on the *London Evening News*, and that became my nickname.

With no Warren Stakes (twelve furlongs) or Blue Riband Trial (ten furlongs) remaining at Epsom, in April the contenders' options coalesce into a limited number of Epsom trials, of which Sandown's Thresher Classic Trial (ten furlongs), the Chester Vase (twelve furlongs) and the Dante Stakes at York (ten and a half furlongs) are usually the most informative.

Crossed wires in the Whitbread

Sandown's late April meeting is a Londoners' bonanza, with not only a string of good-class Flat races, including the Sir Gordon Richards Stakes over ten furlongs, but the Whitbread Gold Cup, the last major steeplechase of the season.

The Whitbread has long been a favourite race, but it's one in which the idiosyncrasies of the Sandown track seem to play a bigger part than in similar races elsewhere. At Sandown, the jumps course has two separate finishing lines, so that horses coming home over fences approach from a different angle to those on the hurdles track. This strange alignment often results in horses running about across the track and it is rare for a Whitbread to be concluded without some erratic courses being taken by the principals. Indeed, two recent Whitbreads have resulted in disqualifications. Both Cahervillahow (set aside in favour of Docklands Express in 1991) and Givus A Buck (demoted to give

Topsham Bay a second success in 1993) had been worthy winners. Intriguingly, in winning his first Whitbread in the year between the two altered verdicts, Topsham Bay himself pursued a wayward course, but luckily just avoiding banging into Arctic Call, his closest challenger, otherwise there would have been three successive disqualifications.

Right at the end of the month, Ascot plays the overture for the Guineas meeting at Newmarket with its own two-day affair, beginning with a night-time card over jumps and continuing with Victoria Cup day on the Flat. Here occurs another of those rituals that herald the imminence of the summer season: in the winter, Ascot uses a parade ring in front of the enclosures for the jumpers, but Victoria Cup day signals the return to the big, shady paddock away to the end of the Members' enclosure.

There are few Ascot days which provide less than average fare, and this spring meeting, which includes the two-mile Sagaro Stakes for older stayers aiming at the Ascot Gold Cup at the Royal meeting, also features the Garter Stakes. A two-year-old race so early in the year may not seem particularly significant, but the Garter Stakes has had a number of notable winners, with Generous, the 1991 Derby hero, holding pride of place. Paul Cole's colt made a winning debut in the Ascot juvenile event in 1990, and by the time he returned there to a wide-margin success in the King George VI and Queen Elizabeth Diamond Stakes, he had tasted victory not only at Epsom, but also over Suave Dancer in the Irish Derby.

May

The arrival of spring in all its glory and the successive weeks at Chester, York and Goodwood promise much, but so often mean the end of the road for young hopefuls who prove just short of what is required.

Northern lights

Chester in early May is one of the year's bright spots in the north; indeed, for ladies from the surrounding area, it's a fair imitation of Royal Ascot (of course without formal dress for men, who would look silly downing their pints in morning suits). Not only does the tight little track within the walls of the old city of Chester attract massive crowds, so that the County Enclosure is invariably sold out on all three days in May, but the atmosphere generated is as enthusiastic as you would encounter at any major meeting throughout the country.

Chester's location, twenty miles from Liverpool, ensures good attendances; indeed, considering the population in and around towns like Manchester and Liverpool, it seems amazing that the only two high-class Flat racecourses in the area are Haydock, which stages good meetings under both codes throughout the year, and the much less used Chester, which of course stages only Flat meetings. Manchester's long defunct Castle Irwell track was once the home of the November Handicap, but dreary weather often made the final meeting of the Flat season an endurance test.

Before Aintree gave up Flat racing many years ago, it too suffered from the climate – during the very hot summer of

1969 I can remember Liverpool staging a July fixture which was ruined by very hard ground, and two- and three-runner races were the norm – but I used to enjoy races like the Union Jack Stakes at the Grand National meeting. Liverpool, too, was appropriately the starting point for Red Rum's great racing career, which brought three wins and two seconds in successive Nationals from 1973 to 1977. The old trooper, still regularly paraded before the Grand National, as he was again in 1994 at the age of twenty-nine, made his two-year-old debut in a Liverpool seller in which he dead-heated for first place. In those days he was trained by the former jump jockey Tim Molony and ridden by Lester Piggott.

Chester in May, though, offers the excuse for some spring enjoyment. The Chester Cup may not be the best-class stayers' race of the season, but the spectacle of about twenty horses hurtling twice round the full circuit of Chester, negotiating the sharp bends before winding up for a final surge down the 250-yard home straight, brings one of the biggest cheers of the season.

If the Mancunians and Liverpudlians latch on to Chester for their early-season delight, across the Pennines the York May fixture attracts equally good crowds, and again the ladies' outfits are an integral part of the meeting's appeal. On the track, though, there is serious business being done, with the Dante Stakes always offering significant clues to the possible outcome of the Derby just three weeks later.

The best things about this York fixture and the later, more important one in August are the uniformly high quality of the racing, and its variety. In May, there are high-class three-year-old races for both colts and fillies, and also Group races for sprinters and stayers. Two-year-old events here also often have significance for the immediate future, and Royal Ascot winners regularly make their debuts (usually winning ones) at York in May.

If the atmosphere at the two meetings is in some ways similar, the tracks could hardly be more different. The tight, narrow, Chester circuit on the Roodeye contrasts starkly with the wide-open spaces of York's Knavesmire, which has a run-in of four furlongs and a straight six-furlong track. Even two-mile races do not involve a full circuit, the horses simply tacking across the middle of the Knavesmire to the end of the back straight.

Down south to the South Downs

After York, the racing circus travels back south, perhaps stopping off for Newbury's weekend meeting which features the Lockinge Stakes before taking in the final Derby and Oaks trials at Goodwood. The Predominate Stakes and the Lupe Stakes, both over ten furlongs, are just about the last chances for Epsom candidates to reveal their potential.

Some of the tinkering with old-established races has, I'm sure, been counter-productive. I cannot believe, for example, that there is any merit in the reduction in the distance of the colts' race, the Predominate Stakes, from a mile and a half to a mile and a quarter. The last time the Predominate unearthed a Derby winner was when Troy won both races back in 1979, and it was only in those final stamina-sapping two furlongs of the Goodwood trial, then staged over the full Derby distance, that he was able to assert his superiority.

Still, that sort of technical niggle cannot spoil the pleasure of bright spring days on the Sussex downs. Goodwood is Britain's most scenic track and the view from its shining modern grandstand, either across the track and over the downs, or behind the stands across to the Sussex coast and the English Channel, is a treat to the eye. Provided, of course, that there *is* a view: sometimes the weather does its best to defeat the spectacle, and if a sea fret comes in, it is rare for it to depart before racing is called off. Some May meetings at Goodwood have been ruined by rain, and even more galling was the evening meeting in June 1992 which proceeded to its conclusion with barely the last 100 yards of each race visible from the stands.

By this time of the year, the evening schedule is well under way. While Windsor relies on the revenues from its regular Monday nights, other courses split their summer dates between day and evening fixtures. The increased coverage of lesser meetings by Sky Sports, in a two-hour programme of eight races from two night meetings, has added to the popularity of evening racing. It was only in 1993 that betting shops were first allowed to remain open in the evenings. Gradually, shops found they were getting better business, and from May to August, that aspect of betting shop coverage is now in full swing.

Whitsun bonanza

The changes to the old Whitsun holiday have had some effect on racing, but what is now officially the late spring bank holiday is still a busy weekend for horse racing. Most intriguing of the Whit weekend fixtures is the two-day jumps meeting at Cartmel, a sharp circuit on the southern tip of Cumbria, where crowds in excess of 16,000 are common-place.

Cartmel boasts no permanent stand, and viewing is difficult from most vantage points. The favourite spot is in the middle of the track; indeed, the temporary stand is actually built inside the main circuit, only coming into the more usual relationship with the action when the horses turn for home after the final obstacle. Then they cut across the centre along a short straight to finish in front of the stands. Before and after racing, massive traffic jams have to be endured. Often the racing is of a modest nature and the ground can ride very firm, but this anachronism of a meeting holds typical British charm and enjoys an enduring popularity.

June

Epsom and Royal Ascot dominate the first half of this month, which also signals the end of the jumping season that began way back at the beginning of August. On the Flat, the number of meetings then slackens off for a while, offering a little breathing space for many stables and professionals in the sport.

Seaside sports

It is during June that the seaside tracks, Yarmouth, Brighton and Redcar, begin to stage regular fixtures. Brighton's track, up the hill from the town, is, like Goodwood, subject to the occasional sea fret, but when the sun shines, the holiday-makers swell the crowds. The course itself, termed a switchback, is not the easiest for an inexperienced jockey, and when Pat Eddery or Frankie Dettori spend a day there, they always seem to come back with at least one winner.

Yarmouth deserves its sobriquet Newmarket-on-Sea, as it is really only easily accessible from racing's Headquarters. Even from Newmarket, Yarmouth is a longish journey, but sensible race conditions make it an ideal starting point for many highly rated young horses on their way to more exacting assignments at the bigger tracks. The view from the stands here tends to be partly obscured by caravans parked inside the corporation-owned circuit; however, the fish in the restaurant is excellent and many racing journalists enjoy an enforced early holiday in one of the many cheap local hotels when their agenda includes two or three days in Yarmouth.

Redcar, at the top of Yorkshire (officially it's now Cleveland, though not for much longer), is a holiday centre for the north-east, and while the attendances nowadays do not match those of thirty years ago when the Vaux Gold Tankard and the Zetland Gold Cup were important handicaps, often targeted by southern trainers like Arthur Budgett, the track has enjoyed a revival under the guidance of its chairman Lord Zetland. I remember sitting next to him at a racing lunch in the late 1980s when he told me of his plan to stage a big-money race at his track. His dream became the Racecall (now Tote) Gold Trophy, with £100,000 guaranteed prize money.

This race was based on a novel scheme with the aim of giving small stables the chance of taking on the big boys on more equal terms than is usually the case in such valuable events. The idea was to devise a structure of weights based on the median (middle) price of all the yearlings of individual stallions sold at auction at major sales arenas throughout the previous year. For example, if a stallion had been represented by five yearlings, which had cost respectively (in guineas, 1 guinea being £1.05) 10,000, 8,000, 7,000, 4,000 and 2,000, the median figure would be 7,000 guineas. The lower the median figure, the less weight any horse by that stallion would carry in the Redcar race, which was for two-year-olds. Penalties for wins in certain classes of race were also applied, while the most interesting aspect, for the small stables, was a sliding scale of bonuses payable according to the number of two-year-olds in respective stables at a certain date.

The realization of Lord Zetland's dream immediately attracted tremendous interest, not just from smaller stables, but also from some of the bigger ones. Entries were huge, usually exceeding 500, and each running attracted a maximum line-up.

Zetland's brainchild came of age in 1993 with the success in the race of Cape Merino, a filly trained by Beverley-based Alf Smith who was better known as a handler of low-grade jumpers. Alf produced Cape Merino in fine shape to beat the high-class sprinters Risky and Bid For Blue as well as twenty-three other hopefuls in the six-furlong race. The first prize was a massive £84,840 and the Smith stable also collected the maximum bonus of £60,000 as Cape Merino had been the only juvenile in his stable at the time qualification for any bonuses was calculated.

Lord Zetland's perspicacity in devising a single race based on making available better opportunities for owners of limited resources led to further action on the same lines by the Jockey Club, and a series of Median races for two- and three-year-old maidens is now well established in the racing programme. It merely prevents the best-bred, most expensive horses in the top stables farming the smaller courses and has been generally approved by all fair-minded racing professionals.

Newmarket nights

In mid-June, while the smart racegoers are still drinking
their Pimms and champagne after the last day at Royal
Ascot, one of the summer's more agreeable traditions is
being revived on the Newmarket summer course.

The July meeting on this rustic, intimate track is just as
serious as Ascot, York or any other major event, but Friday
nights at Newmarket are much less formal, offering lower-
class handicaps, barbecues and entertainment by old stagers
of the music business like Alan Price and Suzi Quatro. Nick
Lees, Newmarket's clerk of the course, has his detractors,
but his enthusiasm in staging the four or five Friday night
fixtures shows him in a different light. His military background, discernible as he conducts business on the Rowley
Mile, is allowed to slip to the extent that he has even taken
to winter talent-spotting of likely groups for the following
year's evening concerts, which are free to all racegoers and
run on well into darkness.

In December 1993, Lees was discussing the new season's
plans and I recall him telling me about some of the forth-
coming attractions. 'We've got Showaddywaddy,' he said,
and added, 'They're good aren't they?' a question I was able
to answer in the affirmative as I'd seen them live when
former amateur rider Brod Munro-Wilson had them as his
cabaret at a house-warming in London. Brod may have
looked inelegant riding The Drunken Duck to success in the
Cheltenham Foxhunters, but that was polished perfection
compared with his jigging about on the dance floor.

Then Lees put in his googly. 'And we've got Edwin Starr,'
he purred, asking whether I'd heard of him. Naturally, those
of us growing up in London in the 1960s knew all the

Tamla Motown singers; Edwin, of course, had sung 'Headline News' (possibly an anthem for a newspaper man). Such luminaries of the music scene had, however, passed Captain Nick by during his army days. 'I'd never heard of him,' he confided, 'but I went to check him out and he's pretty good.'

Sadly, by the time these words are in print Edwin and the other Newmarket stars, like the summer, will have been and gone; but Nick will be scouring the clubs in East Anglia and London during the winters to come, to improve the quality of those Newmarket Friday nights, which I confess are among my favourite novelty occasions of the summer.

The Pitmen's Derby

You might take a gentle sideways swipe at some of the action in June, but for the Geordies, the Northumberland Plate meeting at Newcastle is sacrosanct. The Northumberland Plate, known in the days when the mines were still open as the Pitmen's Derby, is the one occasion when the Geordies can be proud of their local track, which has been sadly neglected over many years as its future has been called into question. This two-mile handicap is a better-class version of the Chester Cup, attracting good stayers just short of the top rank. The crowds fill the ancient stands and several other decent races are staged during the two-day fixture, including the Gosforth Park Cup sprint on the Friday night.

In 1993, the weather for the Friday night meeting before the Plate was awful, rain drizzling down and the temperature unseasonably cold for a midsummer evening. As I perused the racecard before the meeting in my room at the

Gosforth Park Hotel, just a short walk from the track, I noticed that one of the debutants in the two-year-old maiden race was owned by Pin Oak Stud – a name that conceals the identity of one of the more interesting and vivacious characters in the racing and breeding business. Pin Oak Stud is owned by Josephine Abercrombie, a noted beauty from Texas who had had a highly unusual career as one of America's leading boxing promoters and managers. She was associated with more than one champion and renowned as a tough cookie among the various characters on the boxing scene. Now, however, she prefers the mellower atmosphere and slower tempo of bloodstock.

I'd met Ms Abercrombie several times, both at the Keeneland sales in Kentucky and at Royal Ascot earlier in June 1994 when her horse Winged Victory, trained by John Gosden, had been an excellent second in the King Edward VII Stakes behind Beneficial. I'd presumed she'd returned to the States; but eleven days later, here she was in the paddock before the maiden, gathering her raincoat around her to keep off the drizzle as she watched her $200,000 colt Level Sands, a son of the high-class stallion Storm Cat, prepare for his debut. Level Sands was in the care of her other English trainer, Sir Mark Prescott, and I thought it typical of Prescott's minute attention to detail that he had found such a suitable first option for his owner's two-year-old. The betting confirmed my pre-race view that Level Sands was perhaps the pick of the paddock, and when they left the stalls he was 5–4 favourite in a field of thirteen. Everything seemed to be going according to plan as George Duffield took the blue and white silks ahead on the stands rail from the start; but then, in the middle of the track, a dark bay horse went straight past him at the two-furlong pole and

97

drew away to win by seven lengths.

Long journeys home always seem even longer after a disappointing day at the races, so imagine Josephine Abercrombie's feelings as she left Newcastle for London the following morning before making her way back to Kentucky.

Possibly you feel this story lacks something? A point, perhaps? Well, here it is. Sir Mark, that most consummate of professionals, had been as unlucky as it was possible to be in finding a suitable 1993 two-year-old race for Level Sands; for the fellow newcomer that beat his colt, an animal that had cost just 10,000 guineas as a yearling, rejoiced in the name of Mister Baileys and went on to win the 1994 Two Thousand Guineas. It's a cruel world, and a crueller business.

July

With four English Classic races already decided and the Irish Derby also settled, July heralds the part of the season when the older generation tests the ability of the Classic crop. All-aged Group One Pattern races like the Coral-Eclipse Stakes at Sandown, a ten-furlong race often contested by non-stayers that have disappointed in the Derby, and Ascot's King George VI and Queen Elizabeth Diamond Stakes are the highlights of the year in this wider context – especially the Ascot race, which becomes the inter-age mid-seasonal championship.

From Kentucky to the King George

Memories of the King George for me will henceforth almost certainly gravitate to the 1992 renewal, in which the Irish-trained St Jovite followed his twelve-length Irish Derby victory with another wide-margin success against some top-flight middle-distance horses at Ascot.

The St Jovite story began a few years earlier in Kentucky. I was there for the Keeneland sales – which take place, coincidentally, in the days leading up to the big Ascot show-piece. The July Selected Yearling sale is the most important in the world and many champions have been acquired there.

During this particular visit – it must have been in 1987 – I was keen to look at the successful young stallion Diesis who stood at Alice Chandler's Mill Ridge farm. After I had seen the horse, Mrs Chandler invited me to a party she was giving that night at her farm, and when I asked whether I could bring along my friend, the Irish trainer Jim Bolger, she said she'd be delighted.

At the party, attended by many of the top agents, repre-sentatives of the leading Arab owners and well-known American owner-breeders, Mrs Chandler introduced me to Mrs Virginia Kraft Payson, saying: 'You'll get on, you're both journalists.' We did, and when Mrs Payson met Jim Bolger, she said she would consider sending a horse to Ireland to be trained by him. She had horses with Merrick Francis in England and André Fabre in France, but none in Ireland.

Mrs Payson was as good as her word, and after enjoying some success with the first couple she sent, she increased the numbers, and the horses, home-bred at her Payson Stud in Lexington, proved highly suitable for Europe. It was in either the second or third batch that a colt by Pleasant Colony, the Kentucky Derby winner, soon showed above-average ability, and when he won his first three juvenile races, he was clearly a horse with Classic potential. Bolger then sent him to France for his toughest juvenile test, and while he was only fourth behind Arazi in the Grand Criterium, he was not far away, simply being a little one-paced in the closing stages after making the running.

By the spring of 1992, hopes were high that he would develop into a Derby candidate, but a disappointing effort over an inadequate trip first time out and a muscular problem meant he was short of his peak on the day. That he was able, under the circumstances, to finish a strong second behind Dr Devious at Epsom reflected great credit on horse and trainer, and when he met his conqueror at The Curragh in the Irish Derby later that month, he reversed the form, winning by twelve lengths in track record time in the most devastating performance in an Irish Classic until Turtle Island's Two Thousand Guineas romp in May 1994.

Less than a month later, St Jovite came to Ascot for the King George and dominated the field from the start, winning by six lengths. As at The Curragh, he recorded a very fast time, and in that midsummer period he was one of the most awesomely talented staying champions of my experience.

There have been many memorable King Georges, and most of the true champions of European racing have included this great all-aged championship event on their calling cards. Nijinsky, Ribot, Mill Reef, Generous, Dahlia, Shergar, Brigadier Gerard and Sir Ivor all won the race – but then, I had nothing to do with any of them. Certainly joining the party in the Royal Box for a celebratory drink after St Jovite's victory was an experience I'd never expected.

Later that day, my wife and I were invited along to dinner in the San Lorenzo restaurant in Beauchamp Place. When Mrs Payson's son Dean Grimm asked whether they could accommodate the victory party, he was told, 'Only if you bring the trophy along.' So there we were, with San Lorenzo's roof open to London's clear night sky, eating and drinking to St Jovite. Happy days.

Later that year, Alice Chandler and her husband, Dr John Chandler, made one of their regular trips to Newmarket, and I asked her whether she realized the significance of that invitation to her party years previously. 'Of course,' she said, 'but then, it always happens like that.'

Over the past few years Payson Stud has developed into one of the leading thoroughbred farms in the United States. St Jovite was retired to stud there for a short 1993 covering season and is now one of six stallions in residence.

In Yorkshire with the high-fliers

Among the smaller tracks I like attending during this period are Pontefract and Ripon in Yorkshire. Pontefract has always been targeted by smart southern stables because of the large number of suitable two-year-old races it offers during the year. Ripon is another intimate track on the outskirts of that most attractive town which boasts the splendid Fountains Abbey among its historic monuments.

A less restful air characterized one of my recent visits to another Yorkshire track of which I am very fond – Beverley. This was the day in July 1992 when I flew in with Michael Roberts and pilot Neil Foreman to taste the flavour of the South African jockey's ultimately successful title challenge. For Roberts, who in this season would not only take the jockeys' championship but also break the magic 200 barrier in his total of winners, it was a typically busy day, with first lot work for Clive Brittain at 6 a.m. as usual and a ride in the last race at Leicester with a 9 p.m. off time. In between he had seven or eight booked rides and a tight schedule to fulfil.

We joined the plane at a small airfield in Hertfordshire. For Beverley, the planes land on a grass strip half a dozen miles the other side of the town, and the route to and from the track goes right through the busy city centre. On the way there, having first flown over the majestic estuary of the Humber, the taxi driver had a relatively unfraught journey, but the absolute necessity of being in a specific place at an exact time was expressed in no uncertain terms by both the jockey and the pilot.

Roberts was riding in the last race at Beverley (5.00 p.m.) and was also booked, perhaps rather ambitiously, in the six-thirty opener at Leicester's night fixture. Even with a flying start from the last race, and a clear run at least as far as the city centre, his anxiety was soon showing, despite two after-noon winners already in the bag. By the time the car had slipped through the traffic, Roberts was riding a finish worthy of the Derby, slapping the side of the car with his hands as he urged the driver past a line of cars going towards a set of lights.

Soon we were at the airfield, clambering back into the Piper, which then seemed to frustrate Neil with its inability to go any quicker. At times it was hard to tell who was the jockey! As we approached the field near Leicester, clearly with insufficient time for Roberts to make his appointment, he was already clambering out again.

I too made a rapid departure on to the wing, allowing Michael to go through into the first of two cars which were waiting for us and another group making the same ferry journey across country in a separate plane.

Then I waited for Neil to park the plane, impervious to

any thought of danger. Suddenly, I felt a vicious thump across the middle of my back, slumped to the ground and had the shock of knowing I'd been knocked over by the plane's tail wings. A couple of men watching from where the taxi carrying Roberts was just about to leave came over as I gingerly regained my feet.

Immediately I was aware of having badly pulled a muscle in my right thigh, which was considerably more uncomfortable than the point of impact. Neil's face betrayed his own unease, and during the evening once we had reached Leicester (needless to say, Michael did not make the first and was fined for not allowing sufficient time to get there), whenever I saw Neil I hammed up my injury, suggesting a court case might be appropriate.

The following week, at the Keeneland sales, I was still limping; indeed, the effects of the injury tended to recur until October that year, strangely manifesting themselves whenever I caught sight of Mr Foreman approaching from the other direction. He was happy enough when that particular joke wore thin.

Less happy, on that ill-starred July day, was your correspondent. Neil decided to ask me to take an earlier plane back than the one on which Michael was returning home, as he was flying direct to Newmarket. I tipped the last two winners and backed neither. Neil wasn't my favourite man that evening. Needless to say, Roberts collected another double at Leicester.

An eye on Europe

The week before my usual departure time for Kentucky, the Newmarket July meeting is a magnet for visitors from overseas. Several informative two-year-old races speckle the three days' action and the July Cup, over six furlongs, is always significant in helping to identify the champion sprinter of Europe.

Then at the end of the month, following on from two days at Ascot, from Tuesday to Saturday Goodwood stages its summer meeting with yet more high-class sport, among which the one-mile Sussex Stakes for three-year-olds and upwards and the Stewards' Cup, a handicap sprint, provide the highlights. For some of us, it will only be at the end of this week that the realization dawns that jumping is about to start again at the little course at Bangor-on-Dee, close to the Welsh border on the way to Chester.

August

Dog days

The resumption of jump racing in the west country is the ideal opportunity for racing fans to combine a seaside holiday with visits to Newton Abbot and Exeter. Devon's two courses are different in nature, Newton Abbot being just over a mile in circumference and Exeter twice as far round, but the horses which specialize on the western circuit seem to adapt equally well to either. Naturally, Martin Pipe enjoys making a fast start and his willingness to send out horses from his base, however hard the ground may be, usually ensures him a plentiful supply of winners. The quality of racing here is rarely high, and those fast-ground specialists are unlikely to be around much after October, perhaps returning in the spring to pick up the odd race or two.

Things on the Flat are also changing subtly. York's August meeting clarifies further the pecking order among the two-year-olds and races such as the Juddmonte International over ten and a half furlongs and the Keeneland Nunthorpe Stakes over five furlongs vy with the Tote-Ebor handicap, a fourteen-furlong race which is one of the best betting events of the entire year, for pride of place.

These highlights aside, August is the month when racing goes on holiday. Lower-grade races proliferate, while the top animals rest for the busy autumn campaigns which will decide the age-group championships and establish the likely Classic contenders for the following year.

Deauville delights

If British racing has a rather tired look during August, the French actually do go away to the seaside. After the middle-distance French Classics in June, many of the best horses are rested during July and August, and for the entire month of August, when Parisians traditionally go to the coast for four weeks to avoid the heat in the capital, racing packs up and departs to the delights of Deauville.

Not only the horses which will be running at Deauville leave the training centres of Chantilly and nearby Lamorlaye. Some of the animals waiting for the autumn schedule in Paris also depart for the coast so that their trainers can continue to supervise their regimes while they are busy with their runners in Normandy. As for the racing itself, not all of it is run-of-the-mill holiday fare: the odd big mile race, events for emerging two-year-olds and, at the end of the meeting, the local Grand Prix over just a little further than a mile and a half keep the quality going.

Deauville is one of France's most important racecourses, but its buildings are surprisingly simple. The main stands are old-fashioned and largely open to the elements, while even the Members' restaurant, behind the stands, has a temporary, pre-fabricated look.

You are always liable to encounter the occasional English-based jockey here, even on an ordinary day. Until 1994, when Pat Eddery announced that he would not be riding under contract for Khalid Abdullah after the end of that year, the former champion was always liable to show up for a ride on a maiden of the Prince's, and in his last summer's riding in Europe, in 1992, Steve Cauthen and his young wife spent most of the month on an extended honeymoon there.

September

The holidays are over. The days are getting shorter, and colder, and racing is getting going again. As in the spring, time is getting short: for those trainers with candidates for the Arc de Triomphe meeting in Paris, or the Breeders' Cup in the United States, there's just a few weeks to get the programme right.

Second wind: the quality rises again

The main domestic fixtures in September are at Doncaster, home of the St Leger, the final Classic race of the year; Ayr, with its Gold Cup; and, towards the end of the month, Ascot, a three-day fixture which was compiled in the hope of rivalling the Breeders' Cup, but fell some way short of that ambition.

Doncaster in September remains a highly important destination and despite the attempts of St Leger-haters to dilute its importance by getting it opened to older horses, the country's oldest Classic race retains its status. In 1994 Doncaster announced a new sponsor, Mr Godfrey Anderson of the embryonic telecommunications company Tele-Connection, and the race's future looks secure.

Ayr is more of a bean-feast for the locals. The quality of racing is higher than at other Flat meetings here, but compares unfavourably with Doncaster.

Ascot's card on the Saturday of the September meeting was billed for a few years as the Festival of British Racing. It remains a very strong programme, with separate top-class mile races for two-year-old colts and fillies, a high-class sprint race and two valuable handicaps, all set off by the Queen Elizabeth II Stakes, one of Europe's most important mile races of the whole season.

Meanwhile, jumping becomes more established and the proliferation of low-grade Flat racing suddenly ebbs abruptly. We're getting to the final straight for the season and there's little scope for rubbish.

October

It hardly seems more than a few weeks ago that we were looking forward with anticipation to the season's major races, and here we are back again on the Rowley Mile getting ready for a string of important races at the first of Newmarket's two big October meetings, with the Cheveley Park Stakes and Middle Park Stakes, both over six furlongs and respectively for fillies and colts, at the top of the list.

The world travellers might be more intent on looking longingly towards Paris and the first day of Longchamp's Arc meeting on Saturday, when the Grand Criterium is one of the many highlights; but I prefer the age-old English challenge of trying to unravel the mysteries of the William Hill Cambridgeshire, yet another of those cavalry charges along nine furlongs of Newmarket's straight ten-furlong track.

Contemplation: performers and prospects

During this Newmarket meeting the Houghton yearling sale takes place. This is Europe's best auction of quality yearlings, and has two advantages over the summer sales in Kentucky. First, the price level tends to be rather lower; secondly, the horses themselves are a little more developed and therefore a little less of a mystery (one hopes) to their potential buyers.

By now we have almost completed the full yearly cycle. The three-year-olds are getting towards the end of their Classic year, perhaps still nurturing extravagant overseas ambitions, but more probably having proven to some degree disappointing and perhaps being in line for disposal at a horses-in-training sale.

The two-year-olds, by contrast, are likely still to offer some hopes to their owners. Maybe they've won a race or two and look likely to develop further; perhaps they've been able to reach the track only once, or even, if very backward, not at all, in which case final judgement will have to be deferred until the following spring at least. Or maybe they've shown their owners and trainers that despite all the promise on the gallops in early summer, when it came to it they had either no engine, or little inclination to employ it, or both. Those horses could face either a similar trip to Tattersalls' auction across town in their Park Paddocks complex, or, more prosaically, an appointment with the vet's castrating equipment in the hope that drastic measures may produce a similarly drastic response.

For disappointed rather than disillusioned owners, there is always the option of going into the market again. At the Houghton sale which coincides with the first October race meeting, prices are very high, if not quite at Keeneland levels, and demand is extremely strong with the leading international buyers taking the bulk of the attractive horses. Two weeks later, the October open sale is the target of the working trainers with their middle-range customers. The occasional expensive horse is still likely to turn up in this sale, but the buyer with between twenty and thirty thousand pounds should be comfortably accommodated.

For the paupers among the yearling-buying public, there is a final small sale, run in conjunction with the horses-in-training sale when the superfluous bloodstock is dispersed. It was here that Tangognat was bought for 3,000 guineas. With a fair degree of skill on the part of the bloodstock agent and even more luck on the part of his owner, that unpromising prospect turned into a great performer and a reasonable money-spinner.

I'm always amazed just how few of my colleagues ever bother to attend the sales, even when they are staying in Newmarket for the races. I live within fifty minutes' drive of the track so I never worry about staying overnight, but if I were in a Newmarket hotel, I'd make a point of eating at the sales restaurant each night. The action is compelling, especially for the racing man with no previous experience of bloodstock auctions. Seeing which agents operate for which owners, which farms employ people to bid up a horse in the hope of a major killing, and how many lots are actually bought in by their vendors is always fascinating.

From the Arc to America

The Arc weekend for me comprises watching television on the Saturday from the course at Newmarket, a quick sprint back home down the M11 to collect my wife, and the night flight to Paris to get to the hotel in time for bed. Then it's off to the track the next morning to see the Arc and the other great races before a night out with the lads followed by a Monday flight home.

In between the two big Newmarket meetings comes the Tote Gold Trophy at Redcar, where in 1992 the great American jockey Julie Krone rode three winners as part of her European mini-tour. Miss Krone may be physically minute, but she is a strong, determined girl, and a few weeks after her trip to England I interviewed her in the jockeys' room at Belmont Park racecourse, New York. For a girl, Miss Krone could be said to be one of the boys, and the way in which she joined in the general ragging around which seems an integral part of the jockeys' cameraderie at Belmont (and presumably elsewhere in the United States), she seemed to be ruling the place.

I went back to Belmont Park in 1993, even though to do so I sadly had to miss Champion Stakes/Cesarewitch Day, one of Newmarket's most important fixtures of the entire year; but the quality of sport on offer at Belmont that day, billed as the Breeders' Cup Preview Day, was consolation enough for anyone.

For me, the appeal of attending the Breeders' Cup as one of a fifty-strong English press contingent, whose job generally entails excusing the poor showing of the visitors (the French apart) is only limited. The one I did attend featured Pebbles' great win for Sheikh Mohammed and Clive Brittain at Aqueduct – a great occasion, but generally I'd much prefer a solo visit to Keeneland – or as in this case, to Belmont for a programme of five Grade One races with the added feature of the Breeders' Cup Chase.

For an American track, Belmont has everything, and compared with all its counterparts over there, its track is massive. The stands are immense; parking spaces seem to stretch for miles, and the surroundings are bright and welcoming. Sadly for the New York Racing Association, which runs Belmont as well as Aqueduct, the main winter track in the city, and Saratoga, which stages a highly select, prestige meeting in August, the effects of off-track betting have caused drastic reductions in attendance at Belmont. Still, there was a good enough crowd for that Preview Day and to see such stars as Lure, Paradise Creek and the juvenile sensation Dehere was a real thrill. The Breeders' Cup Chase was also an exciting event, won in 1993 by Bruce Miller and his jockey daughter Blythe, who had travelled over to win a race at Cheltenham the previous winter.

Having enjoyed the Chase – in reality a race over rather insubstantial hurdles – it was a disappointment to learn that Breeders' Cup Inc., the management arm of the Breeders' Cup races, had decided to drop it from the 1994 programme of races. Jump racing in the United States is nevertheless, I'm assured by Virginia Kraft Payson, in a very healthy state and reaping the benefits of national television coverage.

111

The Breeders' Cup Preview Day fell rather nicely for another major event which was being staged in Toronto, Canada, the following afternoon. The Woodbine track, which in 1994 was being remodelled at a time when Canada's racing was in some turmoil under the new government, stages the Rothmans International over a mile and a half on the turf. Over the years many European horses have run well here. Snurge, the present record-holder for prize money won among European horses, is a previous winner and in 1993 the French horse Husband came home a long way clear.

The Flat's final fling

Meanwhile, back home at Headquarters, the Champion Stakes and Cesarewitch conclude a meeting which also features the Dewhurst Stakes, possibly the most significant of all juvenile races with the following year's Classics in mind.

All that's left of the Flat season now is the Racing Post Trophy at Doncaster, a mile race for two-year-olds, but this event has been less reliable as a Classic guide than the Dewhurst.

Now, too, the pulse of jumping quickens. Already Cheltenham is well into its schedule; Kempton also is away with the Charisma Gold Cup Chase and even Newbury is divided in its allegiance between the two codes. As the month ends, all that remains for the Flat is Doncaster's November Handicap and the prospect of four months' all-weather racing. We've come almost full circle.

November

Whoever dreamt up the idea of a final turf Flat fixture at Folkestone on the Monday after the end of the Doncaster November meeting must have been either a sadist or an idiot.

Folkestone in the rain is bad enough for jumping, but after a year with horses chewing up the ground, a card with dozens of runners merely adding to the damage makes little appeal, least of all for would-be spectators, who by now are ready to see some jumping stars make their return to action.

Autumn glories

This is the month of some of jumping's best, most revered races. At Cheltenham there's the Mackeson Gold Cup and at the end of the month Newbury's Hennessy Cognac Gold Cup, which often indicates the way the balance of power in the steeplechasing division may begin to shift as the season gathers momentum.

Around now you are as liable to see a good jumper begin his season at Sedgefield as at Newbury. Sedgefield is a marvellous little track among the hills in the middle of County Durham. It's liable to get very cold in midwinter, but on more temperate days the crowds gather and the intimate nature of the course – even if the turf sometimes seems to dissolve into a sea of mud or just plain dirt – draws the racegoer closely into the action.

The standard of racing is by now very strong. The early-season animals have no chance of competing, and there is particular interest in watching out for former Flat racers as they make their early, perhaps halting, steps over hurdles, and for the progress made in novice chases by the previous winter's high-class hurdlers.

December

By now the weather may be taking its toll on fixtures. Some very entertaining sport will be offered during the month at Chepstow, where the Coral Welsh National, on the day after Boxing Day, is always a major draw, as is Wetherby's Castleford Chase meeting the same afternoon.

Wetherby, close to the A1 in North Yorkshire, is one of the best tracks in Britain. It takes a good horse to win the average race there and the Castleford Chase usually goes to one of the three best two-mile steeplechasers in the country.

Ascot has a good pre-Christmas meeting, but the year ends emotionally (if not exactly by the calendar) with the two-day Festival at Kempton, sponsored by that great racing philanthropist George Ward, whose Tripleprint, BonusPrint and BonusFilm trademarks adorn so many races through the year.

The jewel in George's crown is the Tripleprint King George VI Chase, the race in which the legendary Desert Orchid truly left his mark on jump racing. The great grey is now celebrated by a statue near the entrance to the course at Kempton, and the largest crowds of the year throng in to enjoy the racing and help digest the previous day's over-indulgences.

*

So there you have it: the racing year, course by course and month by month. You can see just how much there is to enjoy. Travel around and sample the varying delights on offer.

CHAPTER FIVE

The Men – and Women – Who Make it Happen

Dᴜʀɪɴɢ ᴇᴠᴇɴ ʜᴀʟꜰ a lifetime following racing, first as an occasional companion of my father, then as a punter and finally as a racing journalist, I have obviously seen many talents at work, not only among the horses themselves but among the men and women associated with them; notably, perhaps, the trainers who send them out to race.

There would be little point, in a book like this, trotting out the old clichés and reworking apocryphal or even actual events associated with the greats of this or of earlier eras. Better, I believe, to write from personal experience of some of the objects of my appreciation, both those I have admired at long range and those I have known more closely.

Stars of the sixties

From schoolboy days, the names I remember most vividly are Peter Cazalet, Dick Hern, Bill Wightman, Mick Bolton (for reasons I'll come to later) and Peter Poston. Cazalet first came into my consciousness not in his own right, but in the person of his son Edward, who was a regular visitor to the Eton Manor Club I attended in East London. First-hand, or rather, in my case, second-hand contact with one Cazalet provoked interest in his father's horses, especially those which were or earlier had been owned by Prince Rajsinh of Rajpipla. Prince Pippy, as he is universally known these days, is the son of the Maharajah of Rajpipla, who won the Derby with Windsor Lad in 1934, and a Scottish mother. He was one of the first regular importers of potential hurdlers from France, along with the great Ryan Price, and two good ones, Oedipe and Three No Trumps, were passed on to Queen Elizabeth the Queen Mother. It was perhaps fitting that fifteen years or so after my Eton Manor days Pippy, then based in Paris, and I got to know each other better. At that time he was a regular on the Paris tracks, and offered articles about the French racing scene to the weekly racing paper, *The Racehorse*, which I was editing part-time in those days. He showed more than a little talent for writing, producing articles in a flowery style from a no-doubt expensive fountain pen with which he still signs his Christmas cards.

One Monday morning, he telephoned the paper's Battersea office with some earth-shattering news, tidings indeed so surprising that even when his article appeared four days later, they still seemed not generally known. The previous day he'd been at Longchamp and had seen Mr Nelson Bunker Hunt's colt Youth take his final trial for the French Derby. But he'd been more interested to listen after the race in the unsaddling enclosure to a quiet conversation between Lester Piggott and trainer Maurice Zilber. The Egyptian has always been an optimist, but over the years he's trained many top horses, and he was keen to ask Piggott's opinion. Empery,

116

whom Piggott had ridden into third place in the Prix Lupin, was also owned by Bunker Hunt, who was later to be forced to sell all his bloodstock after being bankrupted when trying to corner the world's silver bullion market. Pippy's simple report was: 'Lester says he'll ride Empery at Epsom and he thinks he'll go well.' He added that to get 33-1 about Lester's Derby mount might not be bad value, so we agreed to have an immediate bet at that price. Less than a month later, Empery ran home one of the easiest winners of the Derby at 10-1 while Gianfranco Dettori (Frankie's father) on hot favourite Wollow struggled home well beaten.

It was Pippy, too, who suggested that it might be interesting to look at French horses as possible recruits to jump racing as the Irish market had become so expensive. The outcome of that suggestion will be revealed later.

Cazalet senior forged a wonderful partnership with the Queen Mother from his base at Fairlawne in Kent and it was sad that when he died neither the stable nor his own tradition was kept going.

Another trainer whose name cropped up in those days was Bill Wightman. He remained as the longest-serving trainer until late 1993, and had already been training successfully for many years by the time he came to my notice in the early 1960s when he won a race with a 50-1 chance at one Goodwood meeting. The horse in question was owned by Evelyn Baring of the banking family, who, together with Mr Wagg of J. Henry Schroder Wagg and Major Villiers, was one of the main forces behind the Eton Manor Club. It was during one of the annual summer camps at Ashdown Forest, near East Grinstead, that Mr Baring predicted that success; my regard for Wightman's ability held firm for more than thirty years thereafter, with some justification.

Dick Hern (or, as we at Central Foundation Boys' Grammar School understood it, Bill Hern) became a hero to me and another friend of mine, Sim Galpert, when he took over management of the training of horses owned by Major Lionel Brook Holliday. The Major, as we dubbed him, was apparently a crusty old Yorkshireman in the dye industry whose entry into the local businessmen's club usually prompted several other members to depart. He had a similar effect on a number of trainers, with Geoffrey Brooke and Humphrey Cottrill being among those employed before Hern took over at LaGrange stables in Newmarket.

Perhaps it was the colours – white with maroon hoop, cap and armlets; maybe it was the naming of the horses, each with the same initial letter as its sire; or maybe it was just the manner in which they always seemed to go so well in the big races which made me back Hern's runners with my two bob each way almost without thinking. Even now the names evoke memories. Hazy Idea, a top-class staying filly and daughter of my all-time Flat-race favourite Hethersett; Golden Cloud; Pugnacity; and so many others.

The story of Hethersett is most firmly impacted on my memory because it was during that amazing year of 1962, when my interest in racing hardened, that his great exploits were enacted. He won the three-horse Brighton Derby trial and went to Epsom – with none of my cash, as the moment of awakening had not quite arrived. But reading the next day about a host of fallers, including the well-fancied Hethersett, did induce feelings of regret for the one that got away, especially when it was an Irish horse, Larkspur, who took the race.

The race was also significant in that it gave Spartan General, an Epsom-trained outsider, the chance to make his first jump in public, over the stricken Hethersett, and Ron Smyth duly launched him on a notable jumping career, in which he even added a chase to his excellent hurdles record before going on to be a top sire of jumpers, notably Spartan Missile among many others.

Hethersett went on to win the Great Voltigeur Stakes at York, on a day when I backed him (13–2), Sostenuto (Ebor Handicap, 9–1) and Persian Wonder (4–1) in a treble after playing a round of pitch and putt on my own at Tuckton Bridge, near Bournemouth. Then it was the St Leger; but soon afterwards we learned that Dick – we now knew it was Dick – was going to take over from Jack Colling at West Ilsley. It seemed almost sabotage when Hern's Darling Boy beat Hethersett in the Jockey Club Stakes at Newmarket the following spring, when the identity of the trainer – the Major himself took charge for a while – was obscured by the name of head lad S. J. Meaney. Talk about illusions shattered; and while there was still one more real champion, Vaguely Noble, to come, he would not be able to run in the Derby because of the Major's death in the interim. His son Brook sold the horse at Newmarket for a record figure. It must have been devasting for Holliday junior when Vaguely Noble proved his own tremendous worth by beating that brilliant Derby winner Sir Ivor in the Prix de l'Arc de Triomphe, but by then we'd stopped caring. Vaguely Noble, of course, then developed into a top stallion in Kentucky.

Like the unfortunate S. J. Meaney (the man who could not win a race with Hethersett), Mick Bolton was a licensed trainer who was not actually in charge of the horses. He worked for Auriole Sinclair in the Lewes yard in Sussex from which she sent out a stream of jumping winners. Fittingly, for a stable run by a formidable lady, the best horse in the 'Bolton' yard was a mare, Wilhelmina Henrietta, and she reached the top flight over hurdles. We hoped she'd win a Champion Hurdle, and one chilly March day I took a transistor radio with me in the hope of hearing the race commentary before we set off in the annual school cross-country championship at Parliament Hill Fields.

The cross-country was not my event. Bats and balls were all right, but charging up the hill at the start of a three-mile slog through mud was less than inviting. Still, my calculations showed we'd probably get back from the race in time to hear the Champion. For a bet, I did manage to breast the hill after the start in the lead before fading into a creditable (for me) tenth of ninety-six, and indeed did catch the commentary in which Kirriemuir (50–1) made amends for his failure when strongly fancied as a four-year-old the previous year.

Wilhelmina Henrietta made the frame, though Miss Sinclair did not get the official recognition, for it was in the days before women, thanks to the efforts of Florence Nagle, belatedly earned the right to be officially in charge of their stables. Later, the Sinclair fortunes gradually subsided, although Credo's Daughter gave her and owners James Bolam and Susan Jameson plenty of pleasure before the trainer's retirement.

The last star trainer of that era for me was the one-time Essex butcher Peter Poston, who trained a few scrubby animals on the outskirts of Newmarket, from where he operated a highly profitable and at the time perfectly legal scam of sending horses as far as possible to the races, simply to collect the generous travel allowances which were current at that time. Thus, for every Hamilton Park, Ayr or Carlisle fixture, the box would load up and Poston would collect several hundred pounds. It was probably almost entirely because of Poston's strategy that the Jockey Club withdrew travel allowances, hastening his departure from the scene. One year, though, he actually had a little two-year-old, called Pigeon's Toes, which habitually made the frame each time he ran – and that was at least once a week.

Still in the 1960s, another name to conjure with was John Meacock, who ran a stable from Hampshire many of whose inmates had Arabic (or was it Turkish?) names. They generally used to trot round the back in their races, but one year he had a colt good enough to finish close up in a maiden; immediately he announced that the horse, called Vakil Ul Mulk, would 'run' in the Derby. After that, his appeal as champion of the rubbish end of racing was lost.

The warhorse and the window-cleaner

If you were a female garage proprietor (or at least had a single petrol pump on the beach at Sandbanks, near Poole Harbour), were in your seventies and a little absent-minded, perhaps the last thing you would want to do would be to own and train horses. But that was the choice of the amazing Louie Dingwall, a crusty old warhorse who each winter used to drive her boxful of horses down to Cagnes-sur-Mer, where she once shocked everyone by winning the local Grand Prix (des Alpes Maritimes) with a veteran horse called Treason Trial. Later, Louie used to recall those happy days, and also the fact that in his youth she once employed the top National Hunt trainer Gordon (not Sir Gordon) Richards.

Her tiny yard was a few steps from the shore in one of the

most select holiday spots on the south coast. Here, throw-outs from some of the big stables would come to experience the combination of sun, sea, sand and Louie's quirky talent – and it tended to improve them. When we met she had a young apprentice, Gary Old, blessed with a cheery manner and a happy-go-lucky temperament. Sometimes in the summer, when Louie hadn't got many horses, he'd work on the deck chairs at the resort; but when he rode, he was a talented young man. Paddy Butler, now training in Sussex, was another of Louie's discoveries.

I used to enjoy looking through the sales returns the day after any of the sales, and one day could not believe my eyes when I saw that a winning three-year-old colt called Princehood had been sold for just 360 guineas at Doncaster. Princehood, a son of Princely Gift, was a wide-margin winner of a Beverley maiden on his first of three outings and was being sold, unusually early it seemed, out of Atty Corbett's stable. Mrs Dingwall was reported as the buyer, and when I rang congratulating her on the bargain buy, she asked if I knew anyone who wanted him. In the end a syndicate was formed in which a disparate group participated, including people from the *Daily Telegraph* and habitués of Mecca's Fleet Street betting shop, among them band leaders Trevor Halling and Chris Allen. Chris, still a keen racegoer, has kept on with the band work, but Trevor now writes for the *Sporting Life Weekender* as Hot Gossip, and without doubt the link with Mrs Dingwall and Princehood led to his altered career.

The horse did quite well, collecting a place or two, but with some of the syndicate members – in typical syndicate fashion – wanting a move, the relationship with Mrs Dingwall ended. So the horse went north to Middleham and the Kingsley House stables, now celebrated as the base of the north's star trainer Mark Johnston, but then home of the selling-plate king Ken Payne. To the extent that we'd established Princehood as little more than a selling horse, this was appropriate; but Ken, known as Window in celebration both of his surname and of his former profession as a window-cleaner, was a bit of a lad. The horses tended to get it wrong when you and the market thought they'd get it right. Ken's jockey John Curant was easily the hardest hitter in the weighing room, something difficult to imagine now when you see his smiling face as he works on his girlfriend Sue Walsh's clothing stall at the major meetings. Indeed, the joke was that while some jockeys smoothed down their mounts' sides to try to eliminate the weal marks, John took out a tube of Polyfilla.

Princehood did win a race; indeed, when we sent him up to Lanark for a handicap, the Royal Scots Dragoon Guards Cup, it was just two days after a moderate effort in a Doncaster seller. The Lanark race was being shown live on BBC television, Princehood was a 14–1 chance, and he proceeded to make all the running, setting a track record for the five furlongs in the process.

I'd first met Kenny when he started training in the New Forest. But with plenty of winners, he gravitated to a larger stable, spending the nights in London trawling for potential owners as skilfully as any trainer before or since. The string of hairdressers, restaurant owners and other businessmen may not have lasted long, but if they could pick up the tab for a while on a selling plater, well and good.

One amusing story from the Payne days concerns the time he had two runners in a four-horse affair at Warwick in a two-year-old seller. He booked Lester Piggott for one and

John Curant, then a five-pound claimer, partnered the other. Lester was alarmed beforehand to find out his was not the expected winner, and when Curant sailed home clear, not only Lester but half the punters in England were screaming.

Both Mrs Dingwall and Ken Payne went out of racing soon after this time: Mrs Dingwall, who by now had very limited vision, into honourable retirement and Payne to Florida, from where he dabbled with training before dropping out of sight.

The Dickinson magic

One day at the *Daily Telegraph*, the telephone rang: Michael Dickinson, then still a fairly young jockey riding for his father Tony at their base at Gisburn near Clitheroe, wanted to have a chat. It seems he was a regular reader of *The Racehorse*, hardly surprising in that his great pal Walter Glynn was a regular fearless – indeed, almost libellous – contributor. The calls became more regular (often he'd phone immediately after getting out of the sauna) and gradually Michael took to asking me whether I thought certain horses might be better served running in this race or that.

It was in this period that the idea came up of sending 'Dad' as he called him with great affection, to New Zealand to buy jumping prospects, as they were much cheaper there than in Ireland. But then Prince Pippy took a hand. Pippy said he knew of some good horses owned by Malcolm Parrish, then running a massive stable of his own horses in Paris under the training name of 'de Tarragon', that of his head lad. (These days Malcolm, who started life from his father's carpet business in Wood Green, is based with his charming wife Sniff in France, and his beautiful Lordship and Egerton studs grace the approach to Newmarket from both the main routes from London and Cambridge, situated immediately before the July Course.) The horses included two which Michael liked the look of, and when we assessed them in the French form book, it was easy to feel positive about their potential. The two horses, French Hollow and Flying Hugue, were duly acquired.

Flying Hugue was particularly interesting. It was by now late summer and as well as running prominently on the Flat, Flying Hugue, a son of Welsh Pageant, had already raced over hurdles, finishing second in a quite valuable three-year-old event at Cagnes-sur-Mer during the spring. French Hollow was a year older, and such had been his level of ability that he had shared top weight in a Tierce handicap – in those days just short of Group class – and finished close behind Trepan, the horse who later won both at Royal Ascot and the Eclipse Stakes before suffering disqualification on the grounds of dope in his system.

French Hollow immediately showed promise, winning several times before challenging for his main objective, a valuable five-year-old race at Chepstow, which he duly won with ease. He then left the Dickinsons' care when sold for a considerable profit to race in the United States, where he also proved successful.

Flying Hugue's debut was interesting. He was one of three Dickinson runners, two of them newcomers, in a novice event at Catterick open to all ages. As a young horse, Flying Hugue had a light weight, too light for Dickinson to manage himself, so Colin Tinkler was employed and presumably believed that Michael's mount Brother Broncho, already placed over jumps in England, would be the first string. The information that Flying Hugue had also run was not generally available, and when he was offered at 12–1 in the market, it looked too good to miss. Unfortunately, there was a long time-lag before the off and the money got back to the track, but not before Tinkler had walked into the paddock to be told, 'You'll win.' He did.

Among horses Michael bought at my suggestion, the one I really liked was an ex-Luca Cumani horse called Honegger. He won around twenty times and was one of the most genuine battlers I've seen.

Years after the Flying Hugue race, when our conversations were far less frequent, I had one of those feelings that another such incident could be happening. I asked about a particular riding plan, with C. Tinkler again down to ride an interesting newcomer at Leicester. Michael was more guarded on this occasion, but half an hour before the race, he tried to get me in my office in Fleet Street to say, 'It's a go.' Needless to say, I was running late, and had to stop off at the betting shop on the way in. The call was therefore fielded instead by Chris Wright, my immediate boss, who quickly shot across to another shop and backed the horse which won in a a canter. Meanwhile, I was backing something else, certain that Michael's horse wasn't expected. The horse was Wayward Lad, and there was further cause to rue what might have been in his case.

Wayward Lad continued to win his hurdle races, and after a victory the following February at Warwick, I felt I'd seen a certain Cheltenham Gold Cup winner. In those days the Tote had a livewire course rep called Mike Cowtan. I managed to secure 100–1 about Wayward Lad for three consecutive Gold Cups, starting two years on. History shows that while he was a good second to Dawn Run in her year (when my bet was already dead), he won three King Georges at Kempton and until Desert Orchid came along was the star turn among fast three-milers.

When Michael turned his back on jumping, racing lost its best ever jumping trainer – a fact emphasized by Martin Pipe's decision to visit him in the United States, where he is now based, to learn some of his training methods. He wins his share of races over there, but the really good horse which would have propelled him, like English-born Jonathan Sheppard, into the top flight has not arrived.

Irish alchemy, Polish charisma

I first heard the name Jim Bolger from the late Irish book-maker Sean Graham, who said he had some horses with a young man who was going to make it big.

On further reflection, I remembered that a J. Bolger had won the Papermate Hurdle at Liverpool a little earlier with a filly called Beparajojo, and from that point took a much closer interest in his progress.

The story moves on to a few months later. I had been asked to help manage the young apprentice Bryn Crossley, who had just joined Geoff Huffer. Geoff, once a member of the Mungo Jerry pop group, had got back into racing after spells as a cab driver, and was now in charge of the horses owned by Cheveley Park Stud, in the days before they went into the ownership of the Thompson family. So when the *Racing Calendar* came out on the Thursday of the week before the start of the Flat season (this was in the days when the weights were all published at least a week before the actual race was run), I was taking a close look at the handicaps.

Of particular interest was a mile handicap for three-year-olds on the opening Saturday of the season. Bryn, who was entitled to claim five pounds, could ride at seven stone three and it was apparent to me that Ben Hanbury had a potential winner in the colt Marking Time, who had just seven stone ten pounds in the weights. Luckily, when I called – and remember in those days very few jockeys, let alone apprentices, had agents – Ben very kindly agreed to allow Bryn to take the ride, and the three-length success they enjoyed together set the scene for Bryn's marvellous season in which he became champion apprentice.

My working relationship with Bryn did not continue into the following year, but my examination of that particular *Calendar* did have far longer-lasting repercussions for me. For right at the bottom of the weights, almost two stones behind Marking Time, was a horse called Lynconwise. The previous year, I'd noticed him as being a reasonable maiden with David Morley. Now the *Calendar* said he was trained by J. S. Bolger, Ireland. After checking the Irish form books, I found that Lynconwise had actually raced once in a late-season Irish maiden the previous year, putting up a performance much improved over any he'd achieved here. Taking my life in my hands, I called the Dublin yard which was then the Bolger base, and asked him whether Sean had ever mentioned me, as he'd said I should give Jim a ring. The answer was in the affirmative. Then I said: 'You do realize that you have a horse that all you would have to do would be to send him over in a horsebox and he'd win just about any three-year-old handicap you care to contest.'

There was a pause, then a cautious note: 'I know what we're talking about – you know what we're talking about. But if we go on from here – there's to be *no names*.'

It seemed the old-style Irish telephone system had its share of snooping telephonists, and when you looked at Bolger's record already, in that embryonic stage of his career, it was small wonder there should be such interest. Within a few weeks I'd learned of some of his amazing transformations of horses – like, for just a single example among dozens, the horse owned by the Nugent family, in whose yard he was training near Dublin's Phoenix Park. That horse was My Hollow, a daughter of Wolver Hollow who, by the time of reaching her fourth birthday, had descended into running in small hurdle races for Sir Hugh and Lady Nugent from their son David's yard in Lambourn. She was beaten by miles in a poor race at Stratford during May of that year, and was sold for a thousand guineas at Ascot – but then was returned when a stable vice was discovered. The Nugents had little option but to take her back home; then, as a last resort, she was sent along for Jim to train. Her first race was not until September. By the end of that season she'd already won two Flat races; the following year she won three more, including Group races, and was eventually sold to the United States for a six-figure sum. Even then My Hollow's unbelievable story had another chapter to run, as she was later sold in foal to Icecapade for more than $1 million.

Anyway, it was planned to bring Lynconwise to England over Easter, but an injury prevented that plan coming off. Instead he came at Whitsun, and Bolger, never afraid of running horses regularly – he ran a filly called Pigeons Nest twenty-one times over hurdles and on the Flat in one fifteen-month period, reaping I think nine or ten wins – asked whether we could find three races over the Bank Holiday. There were suitable events at Doncaster on Whit Saturday, and at Leicester on the Monday and Tuesday. Bryn was to ride at Doncaster and the outcome would depend on that first race.

Lynconwise wanted soft ground, and although the official going for Doncaster was good, with so much rain around we reckoned we'd be all right. On the way up, there were wet pockets, but when we arrived at Doncaster, not only was it not raining, the windy late spring weather had turned the going good to firm. The horse ran quite well, but was only fourth behind Michael Stoute's Montclair.

The drive back to Newmarket afterwards was doubly irritating, not just because of defeat and the losing of bets, but also because the whole way back the heavens opened. Jim was puzzled about what had gone wrong, as I was, but when he asked What about Monday? I was able to reassure him that the ground there really *would* be soft. Lynconwise had just seven stone seven pounds there, and Bryn, for the first of only two occasions that year – the only other was for his Cesarewitch runner-up Popaway, trained by Harry Wragg in late October – rode at seven stone two.

In the event it wouldn't have mattered if it had been eight stone two: Lynconwise sprinted home by ten lengths at 9–1! For good measure he won defying a penalty in an apprentice handicap the following day when Mark Rimmer, who had ridden fewer winners than Bryn, came in for the ride as Bryn was ineligible.

Jim Bolger had already been collecting major races both here and in Ireland with horses like his Yorkshire Oaks winner Condessa. She was sold to America, as was Erins Isle, each for a considerable sum, and both went on to further success. Along with Dermot Weld, Bolger, too, was to become the dominant Flat-race trainer in Ireland; and first with fillies, then increasingly as the 1980s unfolded with colts, he took some of the most important races in Europe.

I was delighted that major owners like Henryk de Kwiatkowski, Harry Dobson and Virginia Kraft Payson reacted to my introducing them to Bolger by sending him horses, and none of them regretted doing so. De Kwiatkowski won the Group One Prix de l'Abbaye de Longchamp with Polonia; Harry Dobson, a Scots-born Canadian national who made his fortune in minerals in North America, built up a formidable team, usually in partnership; and Mrs Payson, owner of a fine stud in Kentucky and the lavish Payson Park training centre in Florida, helped Jim to a first Irish Derby with St Jovite, who went on to win the King George VI and Queen Elizabeth Diamond Stakes at Ascot.

Henryk de Kwiatkowski, quite the most charismatic person I've ever met in my life, was the son of a Polish cavalry officer, who saw his father and many other members of his family killed in the opening days of the Second World War. Eventually he escaped to Britain and enrolled – lying about his age – as a flyer in the RAF. The wrinkled, faded identity paper which gives testimony of those far-off days remains as proud a possession as any of the trappings of financial, business and family success which have accompanied his rise to wealth and fame. After the war he remained in Britain, living in Dolphin Square – nowadays home to Princess Anne, with whose family Henryk has had many social contacts over the years. Then, frustrated at what he and other Poles felt as unfair treatment by the British, considering their efforts in the war, he emigrated to Canada and worked for Sikorsky, the helicopter company, before joining Pratt and Whitney, who make the engines for Boeing aircraft, as an engineer.

It was later, when he negotiated a number of major deals,

first in the selling and leasing of 'second-hand' jet airliners and later in the purchase of new aircraft, that he made his fortune. The most notable such deal occurred at a time when TransWorld Airlines was facing bankruptcy and Henryk personally negotiated the sale of a number of aircraft to the Shah of Iran. 'The cheque was made out in my name. The Shah insisted,' was Henryk's proud recollection. He was on his way, TWA was still trading, and the Shah was a long way from the troubles which were to befall him later on.

In the bloodstock business he was even more successful, buying a string of top-class horses, one of which, Conquistador Cielo, Horse of the Year in the United States after winning the Belmont Stakes by thirteen and a half lengths, was syndicated for $36 million.

I'd met Henryk on my first trip to Kentucky, and saw him set a world record price for a broodmare when he paid $2.8 million for Royal Honoree, who was to be one of the first of Conquistador Cielo's choice harem. When she lost the Northern Dancer foal she had been carrying – Henryk had declined to buy the foal insurance – his sanguine reaction to such adversity was a lesson to all. I was rather less sanguine later, following an offer of his which I rather foolishly laughed off. He told me that while Conquistador Cielo was his great hope for the future (time was to show him as only a workmanlike stallion, not a great one), he had another stallion who would be having his first runners the following year. This horse, a son of Northern Dancer, was unbeaten in three races before sustaining a career-ending injury. Henryk said: 'If you have a mare you can send her to him free.' The offer was sincere, but my reply, 'Well, I'm afraid I don't,' closed the door on what could have been a free service from Danzig, who was to become one of the three most valuable stallions in North America. Within five years, his nominations (single covers of a mare by a stallion) would each be fetching a million dollars!

Henryk still has his film-star looks, though now well into his sixties, and whether at the races, at the sales, or on the polo field he is the centre of attention. And there is real courage under the looks, the charm and the business acumen: he still plays high-goal polo with his team of Argentine professionals under the Calumet Farm banner in Europe and at Palm Beach, and at the age of sixty-six took part in a match against Prince Charles's team with a broken leg!

His finest hour as far as the horse community was concerned, though, came when the famous Calumet Farm was sold in 1992 following a sorry period in its history. Calumet Farm stands opposite Lexington airport and its rolling acres, bordered by glistening white rails, and its buildings with their red and olive green livery invariably seduce the visitor to the blue grass country as his plane descends. It was widely expected that Calumet would cease operations as a breeding farm; as Henryk says: 'They all said it would become a shopping mall. I would not hear of that.' So he went along, bidding $17.5 million to secure ownership, and aims to restore Calumet to its rightful place in the industry. 'I would have paid double that,' he said. Knowing him, I'm sure he would. Certainly few people in racing have made a more lasting impression on me.

Henryk and Jim Bolger had many winners together. Bolger, as the 1990s roll on, remains at the top of the tree in Ireland, and it is surely only a matter of time before he makes amends for three successive near misses in the Epsom Derby. Henryk's Star of Gdansk was third in 1991; St Jovite was second in 1992; and the 150–1 chance Blue Judge was runner-up to Commander in Chief in 1993.

A young master

You are often able to tell soon after he begins just how far a person might go in his profession. Not always, of course – perhaps in the cases of Jack Berry, Richard Hannon and Martin Pipe it might not have been quite so obvious; but more recently Peter Chapple-Hyam and Roger Charlton have grasped the opportunities presented to them so well that both took no time at all to produce Classic winners. I have the greatest respect for most top trainers, and Chapple-Hyam's adventurous policy in his first year, when after all he did not have what were believed to be Robert Sangster's best prospects, has evolved into his particular successful approach. Charlton's quieter style is no less productive, and his smooth succession to his mentor Jeremy Tree was achieved so adroitly that nowadays it is difficult to remember that there was any change at all.

David Loder, on the other hand, was thrust into training as a result of a sad event during late 1992. The sudden death of Charles St George caused his brother Edward, who took over responsibility for the St George horses, to reappraise the situation at Sefton Lodge, the yard from which Henry Cecil had trained the animals in the colours of black, white chevron graced by such stars as Bruni, Ardross and so many others. Edward St George offered the job to the youthful Loder, then assistant trainer to Geoff Wragg, who had earlier learnt the basics of his career with Sir Mark Prescott at Newmarket and the English-born Jonathan

Sheppard in the United States.

Loder began with a half-empty yard, taking out his first licence in September, when barely six weeks of the season remained. His first runner was just beaten at long odds. The same afternoon, fittingly at Newmarket, came his first winner, Lupescu, in the St George colours and at 20–1. Lupescu, strangely enough, had been Lester Piggott's first ride on his much-publicized comeback two years earlier. She lost that day in a photo-finish. Now she won a Listed race. As David later said, 'We can only go downhill from here!'

Of course, subsequent progress was entirely in the opposite direction. In his first full season, 1993, he made a quiet start, with a couple of well-supported winners on the all-weather. But he was clearly a little worried, as he conveyed in a call to me in late May 1993, asking whether I'd help with the placing of his horses.

David and I had shared an odd trip to Keeneland the previous July. The plane we were travelling on could not take off from Gatwick because a door would not close, and the entire group had to stay in the airport hotel that night before setting off the following day. Then, because of an early take-off, we had to stop for immigration formalities in a tiny airport in northern Maine. While we waited, David and I – he was working then for Wragg – talked for a while, and he was still a little worried that he might not be admitted, as he had overstayed his visa to the United States when working for Sheppard earlier. He was in the Sheikh Mohammed entourage for Keeneland that summer, and he was later offered a training job in Dubai; but he shrewdly stuck out for a post in Britain and was delighted to accept when Mr St George offered him his chance.

So on that May evening, when the phone rang, I was

intrigued and went along to talk through David's idea. It was soon obvious to me that winners would come whether I, the man in the moon or the organ-grinder's monkey placed them, and sure enough by the end of that first full season he had clocked up forty-five wins (plus one in Belgium) from a team limited to forty by the number of boxes in the Sefton Lodge yard. His single-minded approach will not countenance failure. Of all the trainers I've known, and the few I've mentioned here are among the best, his estimation of how his horses compare with each other is second to none. All you need is a line to other people's, and you should be all right. With two-year-olds, he shows a balance between getting them ready early and maintaining their form through a busy season; with other, older horses he seems to be able to rekindle earlier enthusiasm, as he did with one-time Derby favourite Peter Davies to notch up two good wins in the summer of 1993. Any mistakes he makes are learnt, digested, and as far as possible, not repeated. He's my tip for the top – with or without any minor help from me or anyone else.

Back to the track

For a successful jockey to move into training is not such a rare event; for him to do so and then return to race-riding at the top level is more of an eye-opener. This, of course, is what Lester Piggott has done, in one of the most extraordinary tales racing has to offer.

It's well known that after his first retirement from the saddle and a couple of years' training, Lester was convicted of tax offences and spent a year in prison. On emerging, he showed no sign of being interested in re-applying for his trainer's licence. In those days, I still worked full-time in the *Daily Telegraph* office, and one day in March 1990 a message came down from Max Hastings, the paper's editor, that he had heard from a member of the Jockey Club that Piggott was going to begin race-riding again. The idea seemed utterly absurd. Piggott, after all, was fifty-four years old, and when I phoned to ask him if there was any thought of his riding again, he immediately said no.

I sincerely believe that at that time he was not intending returning to the saddle; but during the following months he spent time discussing things with Vincent O'Brien, who reckoned he ought to think seriously about it. I also saw quite a lot of Lester at the races at that time, so it was something of a bombshell when in early October that same year the news came out of his intention to start riding immediately: Max, unsurprisingly, was not impressed. The only possible way back for me was to try to travel with him on the first day of his return; and thus it was that Lester, Bryn Crossley, who was driving the Piggott Mercedes, and I set off from Newmarket for Leicester races.

There was, naturally, much criticism in the sports pages of his decision to return, especially among non-racing people, but Lester and I wrote a piece together for the *Telegraph* explaining that he felt his experience was a much more important factor than any diminution of strength because of his age. After all, he reasoned, Bill Shoemaker had kept going in America until past sixty.

The barrage of press and television reporters waiting when we arrived at Leicester races that autumn afternoon was astonishing, but Lester was his usual cool self, and when his first mount back, the filly Lupescu, carrying the colours of his great friend Charles St George, was beaten by only a short head, all the old ability looked intact.

As the day developed – he did not manage a win – we began to formulate a plan for our departure, as Lester was not keen to be caught up in traffic after racing. So, when he and Bryn came out for the last race, I was waiting in the paddock and Bryn gave me the keys to the Mercedes. I was to drive it round to the side gate where my passengers would slip in, unnoticed (we hoped) by the media circus.

I quickly found the car and opened it, but then came the first snag. Bryn is perhaps eight inches shorter than I am and about one-third the girth, so it was impossible for me to get straight into the driving seat; and already I could hear the cries of the crowd as the last race ended. In panic and in vain I searched for a couple of minutes before I eventually located the lever which allowed the seat to slide back. Gratefully I edged in.

The next step was to turn on the engine. Large Mercedes cars do not share with humbler vehicles the tendency towards noisy engines, and the first half dozen times I engaged the key in the ignition, it appeared not to work. By now the sweat was pouring off me and it was only as a final impulse that I put my foot down gently on the accelerator. With utter relief, I felt the car edge forward. Still sweating, I arrived at the gate too late to guarantee my colleagues' anonymity, but just quickly enough to head off the main group of quote-hungry media. In the lead was Graham Rock, armed with a microphone and accompanied by a cameraman. My friendship of many years with Rock made it imperative that I put his request for a 'few words' to Lester, but he merely grinned in that mischievous way and said: 'Tell him you've got me exclusive.' Actually, there was no fee involved in those two days' 'exclusives'.

A few yards out of the track there's a garage, and here Lester said: 'Pull up, let Bryn drive.' Thankfully my career as Lester Piggott's getaway driver was over.

That night, we penned a nice piece for the paper and the following day travelled by plane together down to Chepstow, where we believed he would have a winner, as he had found the ideal race for the useful ex-American horse, Nicholas, a good sprinter trained by Lester's wife Susan for Henryk de Kwiatkowski. Nicholas duly obliged, the Welsh crowd went mad and Chepstow made a nice presentation to mark the occasion. Then it was back to Newmarket on the little light plane, and we settled down to write Lester's article on what he felt his success had meant for himself and for other people.

With time very short, I asked him a few questions, carefully noting the answers and starting to weave them into a recognizable fabric. I said: 'Stop me if you disagree with anything I tell them,' went to the phone and proceeded to relay the article to an office copy-taker at her computer keyboard back in Canary Wharf. For a while Lester watched and listened intently; then he began to correct the odd word; then he said: 'Tell them to hold on,' and, taking the phone, sorted out a couple of sentences before handing the phone back. For a while he was behaving like a professional journalist, anxious that his words were exactly right.

That single win may not have persuaded everyone that the Piggott genius was still largely intact, but when he collected the Breeders' Cup Mile on Royal Academy within a matter of days of his return, and when in 1992 he added two Classics on that excellent miler Rodrigo de Triano, he was completing one of the great sporting comebacks. And of course for me it was great fun to be there and participate a little in the beginning of it.

The pursuit of excellence: owners from afar

Arab owners have added an extra dimension to British racing over the past fifteen years, and while certain aspects of their involvement have produced envy and irritation in some quarters, by the early 1990s most observers of the racing scene were viewing their presence here more positively.

As long ago as the late 1960s a few Bahraini owners, among them Sheikh Essa Al Khalifa, built up strings in Britain, but their involvement had largely waned long before the Iraqi invasion of their country. The next wave of Arab ownership emanated from Saudi Arabia, spearheaded by Prince Khalid Abdullah, whose first major success was the Two Thousand Guineas triumph of Known Fact, awarded the Newmarket Classic in 1980 after the original winner Nureyev was disqualified for causing interference. Prince Khalid and his son-in-law Prince Fahd Salman, son of the Governor of Riyadh, have been most successful throughout the last decade. The Abdullah colours have been graced by such stars as Arc winners Rainbow Quest and Dancing Brave as well as Epsom Derby heroes Quest For Fame and Commander In Chief. Prince Fahd, whose younger brother Prince Ahmed also raced with success under the Universal Stables banner in the United States, operates on a smaller scale than his father-in-law, but he can look back on the thrilling experience of owning one of racing's modern-day heroes. His colt Generous turned the midsummer phase of the 1991 season into a one-horse spectacular as he won successively the Derby, by seven lengths, the Irish Derby, from the ultra-talented Suave Dancer, and the King George VI and Queen Elizabeth Diamond Stakes. At the end of the colt's Classic year Prince Fahd sold a major share in Generous to his father-in-law and his first foals will appear on the track as two-year-olds in 1995.

The final and by far the most important major group of Arab owners to appear in racing here has been the Dubai-based Maktoum family, headed by Sheikh Maktoum Al Maktoum, now ruler of the Emirate, and his brothers Sheikhs Hamdan, Mohammed and Ahmed Al Maktoum. Anyone at all conversant with the international bloodstock scene, especially the major sales of yearlings and breeding stock at Keeneland and Saratoga in the United States during the 1980s, will have been aware of the Maktoums' impact. Keeneland especially had always been the premier source of talent for owners keen to race for Europe's top prizes, and once Vincent O'Brien had identified the stock of the great stallion Northern Dancer as having Classic-winning potential, Robert Sangster, his main owner, made regular trawls of the July yearling sale's most appealing candidates. O'Brien had trained Nijinsky for the mineral tycoon Charles Engelhard during 1969 and 1970, and the exploits of that last winner of the Triple Crown had a marked impression on both the trainer and Sangster. Within a few years The Minstrel, another Northern Dancer colt, was winning at Epsom in Sangster's silks and the owner, seemingly in a monopoly position, appeared impregnable by the end of the 1970s.

But then the Maktoums arrived – first with a few minor horses in Britain, bought on the advice of the late Dick

Warden, and gradually with progressively more expensive acquisitions. By the early 1980s, they were committed Keeneland regulars, and each July they, in competition not only with Sangster but also with some American high-rollers and the leading Saudi princes, were forcing prices for the best-bred yearlings ever upward. Even such dramatic flops as the notorious Snaafi Dancer, bought for the Maktoums at $10.2 million but unforthcoming either in training or at stud, could not halt the spiral, and when Sangster was pushed to a world record $13.1 million in 1985 to secure Seattle Dancer, who was to be only marginally less disappointing than Snaafi Dancer, there was only one way for the market to go. The head-to-head battles gradually receded, with the rival groups (especially the Sangster and Sheikh Mohammed camps) gradually reaching accommodations, and bidding duels became, except in increasingly rare cases, ancient history.

This is not to say that Keeneland is no longer valid as a source of talent; just that the prices are more in keeping with what can be earned on the track, rather than a function of what a demand-led stallion market dictates. A direct result of the fall in yearling prices has been a levelling off in stallion covering fees. A top stallion nowadays might command (in exceptional cases) a fee of $50,000 or a little more, and his owners might therefore feel the need to increase the number of mares he services. Nowadays some stallions cover upwards of a hundred mares each year, compared with the historical norm of forty. It is a delicate balance, and the threat of premature sterility if a stallion is over-used is always present.

The Maktoums soon emerged as major players in Britain. All three senior brothers and their younger brother Ahmed, who operates in conjunction with Sheikh Mohammed through his Darley Stud Management Group, have won major races; indeed, with very large strings to represent them on the track, and a band of high-class broodmares to visit their stallions, it would be surprising if they did not.

'How many things are as beautiful as a horse?'

Over the years, I have found it much easier to develop a number of working relationships with racing professionals and personalities away from the racecourse in Britain. This has been easiest in the relaxed atmosphere of the Keeneland sales ring in Lexington, Kentucky. There, in mid-July, the heat can be unpleasantly humid, but as you travel around the barns which house the beautifully prepared yearlings awaiting their turn in the arena, you are always likely to encounter a top trainer, an agent, the odd film star – or, indeed, bump into Robert Sangster or Sheikh Mohammed as they check their personal shopping lists. While my wife Gill is not the world's greatest horse fan, she did come to Keeneland with me a couple of times, as a photo of her with Larry Hagman (J. R. Ewing of the *Dallas* television series), now adorning her mother's mantelpiece, confirms.

I first met Sheikh Mohammed at Keeneland in the early 1980s, and during the intervening years he has kindly agreed to a number of interviews which accurately (in terms of his input, at least) charted the course which his ever-expanding racing operations would take. In the early days, the protective nature of his group of advisers made communication a little difficult, but both at Keeneland and then a few days later at Newmarket, with the help of John Leat, his trusted personal assistant, and the astute stud manager Robert Acton, we had a couple of interesting chats. The Newmarket conversation took place more than a decade ago but many of the thoughts which the Sheikh expressed then remain in my mind – and in his, too, I'm sure, for his and his brothers' progression to their present position in racing has been utterly consistent. Moreover, apart from expanding, the personnel in the entourage has been remarkably static, confirming the impression that loyalty is one of his most important qualities.

The thing that intrigued me then, and would still do so now without all the evidence of what has happened during that time, was: Why had the family wanted to take such a prominent role in horse racing at all, and especially why in Britain?

Sheikh Mohammed and his brothers clearly had a deep affection for Britain and, as he says, the British people, and they found the racing here interestingly varied and full of tradition. Tradition is just as great a motivation for Arab people as it is for the British. Sheikh Mohammed is aware of the roots of horse racing in Britain. As he says: 'The thoroughbred horses in Britain were descended from Arabian stallions imported from the Middle East. We always had horse racing, even before then, and that is why we love it so much.'

That day at Newmarket, Sheikh Mohammed explained his feelings simply. He said: 'You can put your investment into many things. But how many things are as beautiful as a horse? If you buy a horse you can look at him and enjoy him every day. Suppose you put your money, for example, into a building, you cannot get much enjoyment just looking at it.' Another emphatic opinion he expressed on the same occasion concerned his plan to develop his breeding opera-tion. 'To do that properly does not take four years, it takes forty years,' he said. When I reminded him of those words at least ten years later, he said, 'I was right, wasn't I?' and, turning to Acton, grinning, he said: 'You see how patient I am, Robert?'

Despite the consistent improvements in the quality of the stallions and mares at his Dalham Hall Stud, as well as at the other studs owned by the family, at times in recent years it has seemed to some people, particularly the more extreme tabloid newspaper journalists, that the commitment of the Maktoums to British racing might be waning. Much-publi-cized absences from a couple of important yearling sales, one in Kentucky, another in Newmarket, were taken by such observers as evidence of that reduced commitment, espe-cially as they had by then become easily the most significant buyers at both sales. This temporary absence was in fact the result of their unhappiness at the situation relating to VAT on bloodstock, which in Britain was applied at a much higher rate than in either Ireland or France. With many hundreds of horses in training, as well as large numbers of breeding stock, the Maktoums were finding the 17.5 per cent VAT rate highly invidious, especially when they could point to a VAT rate on bloodstock of 2.7 per cent in Ireland and 5.4 per cent in France. As they had and still have large numbers of horses in both countries, the implications for the sales companies and racing in general could have been far-reaching and damaging had they ever decided to leave Britain, as the scaremongers implied they were about to do. Their quiet but pointed boycott of that Tattersalls sale predictably brought near-panic to some breeders, who found yearlings harder to sell, and to the sales company, which temporarily announced the decision to move operations to Ireland, fearing dramatic falls in their turnover and commissions. But happily, and almost entirely because of the Maktoums' very subtle stand, something was done – and quickly. Legislation enabling owners and breeders to register for VAT and claim it back for business purposes was pushed through by the government: a wise decision which has further cemented the Maktoum family's support for British racing.

The Godolphin Experiment

Over the past few years, Sheikh Mohammed has become increasingly convinced that the warm winters of the Gulf area offer potential benefits for horses which have been racing during the previous summer season in Europe. Accordingly, at the end of 1992 he sent a handful of two-year-olds from the cold of Britain to Dubai, where they remained until a few days before the spring Classics. Dayflower, a filly formerly trained in Newmarket, was officially credited as the first Dubai-trained winner when Sateesh Seemar, an Indian based in the Emirate, prepared her to win at York in May 1993.

By the summer of that year, Dubai's own domestic racing was being further developed and a significant number of Sheikh Mohammed's horses were donated to the local Equestrian Club and sold by auction to various local businesspeople in the autumn. Sheikh Mohammed's generosity, and his foresight in masterminding the development of an impressively modern racetrack at Nad El Shaba, just outside the centre of Dubai City, was rewarded when large crowds of locals and visitors regularly attended the races there throughout the winter season of 1993–4. Instead of large numbers of 'second-hand' horses being sold within the domestic British, French and Irish markets, as they had been previously, these horses formed the backbone of the emerging horse establishment in Dubai.

More significantly, at the same time, the 'winter holiday' experiment for young European horses was accelerated. The project is called Godolphin in commemoration of one of the four original Arabian stallions which were the progenitors of all modern thoroughbreds. The Godolphin Arabian, like the Darley Arabian (whose name is also used reverentially for the main group of Sheikh Mohammed's interests) was one of those founding stallions and the Godolphin project is managed from Dubai (in the winter) by Simon Crisford, formerly assistant to Darley's boss Anthony Stroud.

Pre-eminent among the pioneers was a group of four two-year-olds bought from Robert Sangster, among whom the unbeaten filly Balanchine and the colt State Performer, who had won at Royal Ascot, were the best known. I was in Dubai a few weeks before their return to England in the spring of 1994 and it was clear that the horses looked happy, sleek and in uncharacteristically advanced physical condition compared with their contemporaries who still were facing a couple of weeks' cold weather back in Britain. It seemed clear that the programme of general fitness conditioning was proving beneficial.

Balanchine was first of the pair to run, in the One Thousand Guineas, by which time she had become a partnership horse, with Sheikh Maktoum Al Maktoum taking the principal share and Sheikh Mohammed the remaining share, managed by Godolphin. She looked sure to have won as she and the Irish filly Las Meninas crossed the line at the end of the one-mile fillies' Classic, but after an agonizing wait, Las Meninas (owned, ironically, by Sangster) gained the verdict by a short head. State Performer's fourth place behind Mister Baileys, Grand Lodge and the Sangster-owned Colonel Collins in the Two Thousand Guineas later that week was another excellent effort, but again, it seemed, a case of so near, so far.

The reimported horses remained in England, lodging in John Gosden's Newmarket yard under the supervision of their Dubai-based trainer Hilal Ibrahim and the day-to-day care of Jeremy Noseda, himself formerly Gosden's assistant before his annexation by Godolphin. Disappointingly, the State Performer Derby challenge was not to materialize, but on the first Saturday of June in 1994, the Energizer Oaks became historically unique – for the comfortable winner of the premier fillies' Classic was none other than Balanchine, trained officially by Ibrahim, but in reality by Noseda with more than a little encouragement and involvement from Sheikh Mohammed himself.

Not only was Balanchine the first English Classic winner to winter in and be trained from the Middle East, she was also the first Classic winner to be ridden by the brilliant young Italian Frankie Dettori, for whom a string of Classic and championship wins will surely follow. As Frankie came in to weigh in after his triumph he saw me, smiled and, by way of celebrating, smacked his whip against the left side of my chest before disappearing. Nice lad, Frankie.

Any feeling that the possible problems of acclimatization would cause a reaction in Balanchine's form were firmly dispelled when she adventurously tackled and trounced the colts in the Budweiser Irish Derby at the end of June. Her margin of four and a half lengths over Epsom Derby runner-up King's Theatre, with the Ever Ready third, Colonel Collins, again filling that place on The Curragh, suggested her to be superior to Erhaab, and considering she was only the third filly to win the Classic this century, her merit is all too obvious.

But, I believe, something more important still was happening at Epsom on Derby Day. I discerned what many more racing fans around Britain's 9,000 betting shops as well as the various racecourses which staged meetings that day noticed – the welling-up of emotion for the Maktoum family in general and Sheikh Mohammed in particular. His Grand Design may still be some way from completion, but his pet project, the advancement of Dubai as a world centre for tourism and sport, had been dramatically accelerated. As we spoke on the telephone again that night, the joy and pride were never far below the surface, especially the thought that the British racing public had been won over. Sheikh Mohammed re-iterated his oft-spoken truism. 'As long as we're welcome here, we're happy to stay and race here.' To the hundreds of stable and stud staff, accountants, shippers and the entire Maktoum management teams, not to mention other commercial breeders who have benefited from the family's presence in Britain, those words will have been music to the ears.

CHAPTER SIX

Changes Afoot

The Jockey Club and the BHB

During 1993, the institutional structure of racing in Britain changed irrevocably. Up to this time the Jockey Club had taken responsibility for the entire operation of horse racing: the licensing of courses and of the participants in the sport, owners, trainers and jockeys as well as officials such as stewards, starters, vets and handicappers; and the making and implementing of the Rules of Racing, together with the running of the integrity services. The Jockey Club, a private body which selects its own members, had governed racing for more than 200 years, and since 1970 had been incorporated under a Royal Charter. However, the 1980s saw increasing unease that such a body should control all aspects of the sport, especially since the financial implications had altered so much with the advent of Satellite Information Services' daily coverage of racing. The resulting debate led eventually to the setting-up of the British Horseracing Board (BHB), now firmly in control of all racing matters apart from discipline and licensing, which remain under the aegis of the Jockey Club.

Those responsible for setting up the BHB made the wise decision, after much canvassing of expert opinion throughout the industry and among Members of Parliament, that the Jockey Club would have a major input into the new organization. Accordingly, Lord Hartington, outgoing Senior Steward of the Jockey Club at the time of the formation of the new body, became Chairman of the BHB. His fellow directors comprised Sir Neville Macready, formerly of the Levy Board, and eight others, representing the interests of the Jockey Club, the Racecourse Association and the Racehorse Owners' Association. Its secretariat is headed by the Chief Executive Tristram Ricketts, formerly Secretary of the Levy Board, and includes directors for racing, marketing, financial control, race planning, industry and training. These functions are exercised through standing committees within the BHB which relate to industry, racing and thoroughbred breeding, training, race planning, finance and racing development. These committees include members drawn from other related groups, for instance the Jockeys' Association and Lady Riders' Association. The requirement that all appro-priate opinion would be represented has therefore been largely fulfilled. The general view within racing, after a year or so under the new arrangements, is that considerable progress has been made, not least in communicating the BHB's attitude.

Licensing and discipline

Many criticisms have been levelled at the Jockey Club over the years, but if the word 'incompetent' has featured in some of them, it has seldom if ever been coupled with the accusation of dishonesty. The decision, therefore, to retain

151

the functions of licensing and discipline within the Jockey Club has been welcomed in most quarters.

The Stewards of the Jockey Club have to rule on such delicate matters as riding suspensions imposed by local stewards and contested by the victims. It falls on the Disciplinary Committee, headed by Anthony Mildmay-White, to decide on these incidents. For instance, a jockey might be found guilty of causing interference by a panel of stewards on a racecourse, who then impose a ban according to a scale laid down by the Stewards of the Jockey Club. If the jockey disagrees with the verdict, he may appeal to the Jockey Club. The Disciplinary Committee then meets to establish the facts, beginning with no reference to the findings and evidence at the original inquiry. At Jockey Club inquiries, the appealing jockey can employ a legal representative to argue his case. Instances of original decisions being overturned are infrequent, although some jockeys have been notably successful in that regard. Declan Murphy, the stylish Irish-born jumps jockey, has appeared several times to appeal against riding bans imposed by local stewards and has had a perfect record on such occasions, each time being exonerated by the Disciplinary Committee. It was a sad day for racing in May 1994 when Murphy suffered serious injury in a fall at Haydock Park, but happily he made a good recovery.

The Licensing Committee also fulfils an important function. Potential trainers, for instance, need to show they have the facilities and the knowledge to be able to train effectively. Such successful licence-holders as the former footballers Mick Channon and Francis Lee had to serve periods as assistants in other yards before being granted their licences, as did businessmen John Upson and Mel Brittain.

Red Face Day – and after

The unacceptable face of the Jockey Club still persists in some quarters, though, and it will be some time before the events at Aintree in April 1993 are forgotten.

The Grand National is not merely an institution with the British racing public; it is among the world's greatest races, and its position as one of the BBC's leading television exports to the rest of the globe cannot be lightly dismissed. In practical terms for racing, too, it is vital that everything works. That single day generates the biggest turnover of any during the year: it is reckoned that up to £50 million is gambled on the race itself, representing a cash value to the government of £4 million and to racing of around £1 million. If, as happened in 1993, the race does not take place, the financial cost is obvious. But in terms of national prestige, the fact that the 1993 Grand National was abandoned despite a number of horses completing the entire course, and despite a red flag signifying a second false start, was even more damaging.

The elaborate measures taken to ensure the same thing did not happen the following year proved entirely successful. A new starting gate, which did not allow horses to get their heads over the tape – the root of the problem in 1993 – and the provision of extra recall measures so that jockeys would not be left in doubt about whether there was in fact a false start were both important. Even more vital, though, was the increased security in the form of additional police presence to counter the possibility of animal rights protesters repeating the confusion they created the previous year, and the additional fencing erected to prevent such people getting anywhere near the track and the horses. All these measures contributed to a trouble-free renewal and showed that a great deal of thought, springing from consultation among interested, knowledgeable groups, had arrived at the correct outcome.

Perhaps even more important in a symbolic way was the effect that a minor sartorial change had on the sensitivities of the viewing public. Instead of the firm-brimmed bowler hat favoured by the old school of Jockey Club starters and indelibly cast in the memories of that shambolic day as the headgear of the hapless Keith Brown, we saw the soft trilby favoured by his successor Simon Morant, who is now adorned by the title: Manager, Starters' Department. The BHB had taken over from the Jockey Club.

The jigsaw slots together

Weatherbys

For many years, the family firm of Weatherbys has been stakeholder to the Jockey Club, and it continues in that role under the new order, although there have been suggestions that its position could be challenged by new entrants to the field. Weatherbys' offices in Wellingborough, Northamptonshire, have been adapted to fulfil the demands made by recent technological advances, and are equipped to carry out their functions of taking entries for races and supplying information on all race programmes to various interested media and other bodies.

Members of the Weatherby family have traditionally been accepted as honorary (non-voting) members of the Jockey Club, and Johnny Weatherby, the young driving force behind the company, which also has a thriving publishing arm, is determined that Weatherbys will remain in its focal position in racing's hierarchy.

The Levy Board

While the Levy Board remains a separate organization, it can only be a matter of time before it becomes an integral part of the BHB. Both Sir Neville Macready and Tristram Ricketts built up their power base here, using the influence exercised by the holders of the purse-strings in any industry, and they will want to retain that power as the industry continues to develop.

With an annual budget of around £55 million to allocate, the Levy Board recycles racing's share of betting turnover into prize money, the provision of improved facilities via loans (sometimes interest-free) to racecourses and the financing of the cost of integrity services, such as the race patrol and dope testing.

United Racecourses

One single transaction in the spring of 1994 altered the balance of racecourse ownership. For many years it had seemed incongruous to some that the Levy Board should own the three courses which comprise the elite United Racecourses group of tracks. So when Sandown Park, Kempton Park and Epsom were put up for sale, officially to augment the coffers of the Levy Board and reduce borrowings, there were several interested parties. The successful bid of Racecourse Holdings Trust, a subsidiary of the Jockey Club, which thus added notably to its already impressive portfolio of courses, including Newmarket, Haydock, Cheltenham and Liverpool, among others, was not universally popular, but there is no doubt RHT have the personnel expertise to maximize United's potential.

All-weather, all year

Over fifteen years ago the Jockey Club, then still racing's supreme ruler, was becoming increasingly concerned at the number of race meetings that were lost to the weather during severe winters. At that time, it had become the practice to reschedule the lost meetings later in the season, but inevitably such rescheduling did not compensate those horses and their owners and trainers who had been frustrated earlier. Moreover, the lost midwinter meetings tended to feature good-quality racing with valuable prize money. The substitute fixtures were generally staged much later in the season, often in April and May when the ground had firmed and most high-class horses had already finished for the season. Thus the so-called substitute races were effectively no substitute for the horses denied their opportunities earlier on, and became instead additional opportunities for those lesser animals who in any case had plenty of chances at the minor meetings already scheduled.

The need for all-weather racing therefore became much more pressing, not so much as an alternative for owners and trainers who had lost opportunities by way of cancelled races, but to maintain Levy revenue for racing. To recap on how the system works: British racing is funded primarily by regular payments from off-course bookmakers. An average of around 1.25 per cent on all betting turnover by punters goes back into racing to pay for prize money, the integrity services (such as the race patrol and dope testing) and capital projects for racecourses. From a total betting aggregate of around £4 billion, the government takes 8 per cent and racing ends with a sum of approximately £55 million a year. With extra revenue from SIS going to the individual tracks, the finances of racing are better than in recent memory. Even a temporary halt in that regular flow of money to racing from betting shops is clearly against the interests of the industry – and, more especially, of the Exchequer, which collects around £250 million each year.

Having agreed in principle to the need for all-weather racing, the Jockey Club needed to make drastic changes to the established order. Initial feelings were that jumping on all-weather might be impracticable and it was accepted that, initially at least, the new action would be primarily on the Flat. But historically, the Flat season had begun with the Doncaster Lincoln meeting in March and ended at the same track's November Handicap meeting in early November. To get all-weather racing during that sacrosanct out-of-season period accepted required plenty of hard canvassing by the authorities.

Several courses soon revealed an interest in developing all-weather tracks. Kempton in the south, and Doncaster in the north, were the original front-runners, but eventually both these Grade One tracks felt that the activity might cut across their existing sport. In the end it was Lingfield Park in Surrey, and Southwell in Nottinghamshire, which developed the sand-based tracks that have since generally managed to maintain a service through the worst of the winter weather.

Then, in late December 1993, Wolverhampton joined the other two tracks, offering the innovation of floodlit racing for the first time in Britain. Unlike Southwell and Lingfield, where the changes to the existing track were modest, to the extent that the old circuits were largely left in place, Wolverhampton's development involved a wholesale change. The old grandstand was left standing more than 300 yards away from a brand new development, which faces a long narrow loop course of just under a mile in circumference. The action is fast and furious, and close to the stands; a strong emphasis has been placed on spectator facilities, and the trackside restaurant has boasted 'House Full' notices for every Saturday night meeting since its inception.

Wolverhampton has begun what should become an industry-wide trend for family attendance. Saturday nights in Wolverhampton are already popular and Richard Muddle, who operates the track, shares his father Ron's enterprise. When I arrived at the track for the first meeting of the new order on Boxing Day 1993, the first two people I saw were Ron and Richard Muddle, busily directing traffic into the car parks. Hands-on management of the first order.

While Flat racing at Wolverhampton, its sister track Southwell, and at the southern outlet Lingfield has progressed satisfactorily, jumping on sand has been less free of controversy.

In the early days, Southwell attempted to stage a series of steeplechases on its all-weather track but these were soon discontinued, and that course and Lingfield used the jumping dates to run hurdles-only fixtures. Initially, the obstacles were simply dark green plastic boards, but these were so easily knocked down that they encouraged careless jumping and all-weather hurdling became a poor excuse for the authentic hurdling over birch on the turf tracks.

Great thought went into the production of new all-weather

hurdles, based more on the French-style jumps. These required much more accomplished jumping, and thus solved one problem; but only to cause another, as gradually casualties at Lingfield and Southwell began to increase. Many believe that it was the modest quality of the horses which all-weather jumping attracted, rather than the hurdles themselves, which led to the increased ratio of injuries to horses compared with turf hurdling, but whatever its causes the injury rate was seen as unacceptable, and in the spring of 1994 the British Horseracing Board announced the discontinuation of all-weather hurdle racing.

The track managements at Lingfield and Southwell were relieved by this decision, partly because of the worry and bad publicity caused by the high injury levels, but also because Flat racing on the all-weather tracks has been infinitely more competitive. Fields have been growing throughout the winter season, and owners and trainers have been delighted to keep Flat horses busy racing for good prize money rather than leave them inert during the winter or sell them before they achieve their full potential.

A side issue concerning all-weather Flat racing and its attraction for betting-shop punters has been the way in which certain horses have been able to compile impressive winning tallies. Rapporteur at Lingfield and Tempering at Southwell have been among the most successful sand horses. Sadly, other potential money-spinners cannot be exploited as the level of races on all-weather is very low. It's bread and butter for the industry, rather than jam for the top animals, but I feel that all-weather Flat racing, twelve months in the year, is here to stay.

Sunday racing

Sunday racing, with betting shops open and betting on course, is upon us following the May 1994 parliamentary vote to allow racing to compete on equal terms with other leisure activities. This development can only augment the Levy and therefore increase racing's prosperity.

Stable staff have been a predictable source of criticism of this move; but already the top stables have been effectively operating a seven-day regime, with regular Sunday runners on the continent. With Sunday cards at present envisaged only on selected weekends, it will be some time before the existing fabric of racing is fundamentally altered; but a large number of courses are clearly keen to stage Sunday fixtures.

The seventh day in Ireland

The Sunday racing scene in Ireland differs from what is envisaged in Britain. Betting shops remain closed and even the on-course facility does not operate, so should there be a second meeting that day, punters at the other one simply cannot get on.

After a good start, Sunday racing in Ireland has settled into a slower mode, although point-to-points are staged almost exclusively on that day, attracting regular visits from the top English jumping trainers. A Nicholson, Henderson, Edwards or Sherwood is likely to be seen plugging through Irish mud in his gumboots on any Sunday between January and May.

Phoenix Park, now sadly closed, was the course most readily associated with Sunday racing in Ireland. Under the stewardship of the enlightened Jonathan Irwin, now teamed at Doncaster with the equally far-sighted John Sanderson, the Park, right in the middle of Dublin, was the magnet for many families on summer Sundays. The management found, however, that picnickers do not necessarily bring much revenue into the tracks, minimizing expenditure by bringing sandwiches and thermos flasks with them. The Park, having already suffered a previous closure, flourished only briefly before going out of business for good at the end of the 1980s.

For one colleague and good friend of mine, however, the Park offered the chance to make his name. The Australian commentator Jim McGrath (not to be confused with the equally professional Channel Four presenter of the same name, who works for Timeform) came over from Hong Kong, where he had hosted a regular television show, to try his luck in Britain. Graham Rock had signed him for the *Racing Post*, and the Australian-born McGrath was soon making an impressive mark with his energetic search for knowledge and information which greatly enhanced the pages of the *Post*.

Irwin had heard McGrath's commentaries in Hong Kong and took the not inconsiderable risk of giving him his first European chance. That exposure was followed by a similar opportunity at Ascot, and now McGrath is widely acknowledged as the leading racecourse exponent of the art, and the assured successor to the great Peter O'Sullevan.

His role as Hotspur on the *Daily Telegraph*, too, has been taken on with typical skill and energy, and he is the easiest of colleagues with whom to work.

A Sunday Derby?

The biggest days for the Levy, when most punters bet, are Grand National day, the Cheltenham Festival in March and Royal Ascot in June. The days when Derby Day was the biggest spectator event of the year are long gone, but prospects of a full-to-capacity Epsom Downs have been much improved by the Commons vote on Sunday racing.

Epsom has been keen to stage the Derby on a Sunday for several years; indeed, the Board of United Racecourses has seen a Sunday Derby as the only true salvation for the meeting, which has steadily declined as a spectator attraction over many years. It may be fine for the guests in the boxes to take a Wednesday off work, and also for the busloads of pub outings; but families are conspicuous by their absence on the Downs nowadays, despite the funfairs and other attractions in the centre of the track. A Sunday Derby, with reasonable admission prices for cars in the infield car parks, would regenerate the event; but before that occurs, a Saturday Derby will probably be tried by the track's new owners.

My first trip to the Derby was as recently as Nijinsky's year, 1970; perhaps surprising as I'd seen the Two Thousand Guineas with my father as long ago as 1954. Nijinsky's year was a very special one, with the unbeaten champion ridden by Lester Piggott and trained by Vincent O'Brien. For me, watching from the old press stand at the top of the Grandstand, it was a thrill never to be forgotten seeing this great partnership swoop on the French colts Gyr and Stintino; but my memory also recalls the massive lines of open-top buses and the crowds which flocked on to the hill from soon after first light to get a view of the race.

Twenty or more years later, most of that part of Derby

day has gone. A Saturday or Sunday Derby will bring much of it back, I'm sure. The logic of enabling people to follow their pastime on the day when they are available to follow it cannot be more obvious. At last, British racing fans will be able to attend on the day when they are free to do so.

Festival Days

The crack

No one has a greater affinity with the festival mood of racing than the Irish, as anyone who frequents Cheltenham for the great March meeting knows. On their own soil this relentless pursuit of 'the crack' takes many forms, from the seaside curiosity of Laytown in August, where there is no course once the tide rubs out the temporary markers, to the extravaganzas of The Curragh and Galway.

One Irish meeting I particularly enjoy is the spring jumps bonanza at Punchestown. It's hard to win a race there, so when my horse Christo finished fourth in the big juvenile hurdle race, it felt as though we had won. On the same day I noticed another four-year-old, Team Challenge, taking on a rather more exacting task than the soft two miles which Christo was asked to tackle.

Team Challenge was running for the third time in four days at the Festival, but not over hurdles. He'd already contested two hunters' events, being awarded the second on a disqualification, and was now in the La Touche Cup, over an extended four miles of the bank course – a real Irish speciality and one without parallel in Britain, where the horses have to land on top of the banks, change legs and spring off again.

Pat Hogan, that noted hunter-chase and point-to-point exponent, knew his horse and while Team Challenge did not win, he jumped the unusual obstacles with great fluency. My suggestion that he might one day become a Grand National horse enticed Terry Ramsden to buy him, and though he did quite well, that 'win' through disqualification prevented trainer Jenny Pitman from carrying out the usual initial campaign which would have maximized his potential, as he had become ineligible for novice events.

Ramsden's departure from the racing scene robbed the sport of a generous if mercurial character. His filly Katies brought him Classic success, while his much-publicized winning gambles ensured that Ladbrokes especially would ever be wary of him. Sadly, their decision to decline his custom preceded a more significant personal setback when the sudden stock market crash of the late 1980s eroded the fortune which he had built up on the basis of a shrewd understanding of the Japanese warrants market.

While Punchestown is an eagerly anticipated festival among the jumping fraternity, the Irish are even more proud of their Galway fixture, which coincides exactly with Goodwood. For six days, sometimes in the afternoon, and a couple of times in the evening, the biggest betting bonanza of the year is interwoven with all-night card games, copious consumption of Guinness and oysters – and a succession of competitive races, among which most of the handicaps include a 'job' horse laid out for the race. The Galway Plate, run over two miles five furlongs, is the summer Grand

National and attracts a high-class entry. The English find it hard to win, especially as for them, unlike in Ireland, steeplechasing has been over for eight weeks by the time Galway comes around.

Galway is followed on the festival circuit by Tralee and Listowel, both tracks where the rivalry between the masters Jim Bolger and Dermot Weld continues blow for blow. Weld, though, usually has the edge at Galway, a track at which Bolger has been relatively conservative since those far-off days when Peter Scudamore rode his first important winner for the Irish trainer as an amateur.

Cheltenham, Aintree and a forgotten hero

The races you remember best need not necessarily be the ones freshest in the memory. Indeed, my most vivid recollection of the Cheltenham Festival extends back more than twenty years. The memory actually begins a few years even earlier than that, when Mr Raymond Guest's striking chesnut gelding L'Escargot travelled to Cheltenham and ran in the second division of the Gloucestershire Hurdle, the novice race which the great Vincent O'Brien had farmed with such skill two decades earlier. L'Escargot won this race quite comfortably, and as he went through his career he became a great favourite.

I was by that time working at the Press Association, and used to speak quite often to John Hughes, then clerk of the course at Haydock Park. John had helped design a race series for second-season novice chasers, sponsored by Wills, with heats around England, plus a single one in Ireland, and a final at Haydock Park in January. The Wills Premier Chase, soon to become the Embassy Premier Chase, became the target for L'Escargot, who following his novice achievements in Europe was sent to the United States to contest a couple of major steeplechases. He won in top company there, and indeed was Steeplechaser of the Year when he came back for the Irish Wills qualifier in which the Dreaper family's East Bound beat him by three-quarters of a length. In those days, heat winners were penalized five pounds. East Bound, a good novice, therefore had to concede five pounds to L'Escargot, who now had the crown of US champion chaser to add to his hurdling accomplishments. I felt he would not only win the Wills Final, but also collect the Gold Cup in which the Dreaper stable had Kinloch Brae to represent them.

So it was with real anticipation that I travelled up to Haydock. As well as backing L'Escargot at 9–4 for his race there – a moral certainty to my mind – I'd also taken 20–1 about the Gold Cup. I reckoned if he won at Haydock you'd be lucky to get better than tens for Cheltenham. I'd also coupled L'Escargot with a horse called Some Jest, who had been backed from 20–1 at the beginning of the week down to as low as 4–1 by the Friday, for the supporting Wills Handicap Hurdle. Ryan Price trained Some Jest and again, I felt he'd be even shorter on the day.

To cut short a long story, a long train journey and a weekend in Manchester, a place which has rarely been on my itinerary since, both horses won. We celebrated just a shade, and then I couldn't wait for the Gold Cup.

As the weeks went by, L'Escargot, originally cut to 12–1 after Haydock, started to drift, and on the morning of the race he was back to 20–1. Naturally, I had to have a little of that, and when I arrived at the track before racing, there was plenty of 25–1, so another 'press-up' was in order. At no stage during the three and a quarter miles did any outcome other than a win for L'Escargot seem likely, and he came home the comfortable victor at an astonishing price of 33–1. In following up the next year, in desperate ground, L'Escargot, at eight, was the first since the great Arkle to win successive Gold Cups, a feat which by 1994 still remained unmatched since, with Jodami failing to pin back The Fellow.

Even if that had been the sum total of L'Escargot's exploits, surely he would have merited more prominence in jumping's Hall of Fame; but his second (or rather third) distinct phase was almost as glorious. His trainer Dan (father of the present top Irish trainer Arthur) Moore was by now into the twilight phase of both his training career and his life, but with the help of his great rider Tommy Carberry, L'Escargot had his attentions turned towards Aintree. He fell on his first attempt, but when Red Rum collected the second of his three Grand Nationals under top weight of twelve stone in 1974, it was the eleven-year-old L'Escargot, carrying just one pound less, who followed him home seven lengths behind.

Many felt that he would never beat his adversary. In 1975, Red Rum was at his prime at ten, while L'Escargot at twelve was not just a veteran, but seven years older than when he scored his first Cheltenham success, five years older than when he won his first Gold Cup. The handicapper tried to put them together, allowing L'Escargot ten pounds more this time, and when the rains turned the ground soft, Red Rum was at a disadvantage. As the pair came to the last fence, L'Escargot's wise old head, by now adorned with light blue blinkers to help him concentrate, nodded; Brian Fletcher, on Red Rum, turned to Carberry and said 'go on' – and so he did, winning by fifteen lengths. Spanish Steps, also a former star and winner of the Hennessy in the same season that L'Escargot won his first Gold Cup, was third, twenty-three lengths behind the winner and carrying fourteen pounds less.

That was one of the great Grand Nationals. When people talk about underrated champions, I always put forward L'Escargot as the one everyone forgets.

Goodwood and the Arc: Lochsong flies

It was in the 1992 Stewards' Cup that the feeling first came through that there could well be a new sprinting star. Ten years earlier, the northern filly Soba had made all the running down the stands rail, and now it was Ian Balding's filly Lochsong who repeated the achievement, barrelling down the same furrow that her predecessor followed, entering the final furlong a couple of lengths clear and holding on to win. There were thirty runners that day, and Lochsong probably never saw another horse once she left the stalls.

Six weeks later at Doncaster, it was the mixture as before, with Lochsong rocketing home this time from twenty-one others in the hands of Willie Carson. When Carson was unavailable a week later at Ayr it was unknown apprentice Frankie Arrowsmith who was entrusted with the mount. Ten-pound penalties are supposed to stop horses, but for a filly like Lochsong such irritations as extra weight, a different (and indeed, inexperienced) jockey and the small matter of twenty-seven opponents make no difference. By halfway

Lochsong was almost a dozen lengths clear, and if she tired a little it was at least as much through having had two hard races in a short time as through lack of stamina.

Ian Balding and owner-breeder Jeff Smith by now knew they had a phenomenal sprinter, and although she had the occasional off day the following season, her Nunthorpe Stakes success at 10–1 suggested that she was the best at five furlongs, even if she could not quite match Wolfhound and Catrail in the Hazelwood Foods Cup over six furlongs at Haydock.

And that brings us to Arc day – to be precise, the 1993 Prix de l'Abbaye de Longchamp and the most one-sided Group One sprint I've ever seen. With Wolfhound again in opposition and Lochsong seemingly hopelessly drawn in stall nine of the eleven runners, she was a 2–1 chance behind the Sheikh Mohammed pair Wolfhound and 1993 Stewards' Cup winner Kings Signet, coupled at 6–4.

But if the draw was a disadvantaged one, nobody told the mare, or her rider. Dettori flashed her out so fast that Lochsong was already six lengths clear after a furlong. She never changed stride and never faltered, maintaining the advantage to the line, where Stack Rock battled through late to take second, still six lengths adrift. On going officially heavy, she still beat one minute for the five furlongs.

Happily the Lochsong story was not yet over. Her six-year-old career began with yet another overwhelming success in Newmarket's 1994 Palace House Stakes on Two Thousand Guineas day and continued gloriously in Royal Ascot's King's Stand Stakes. So often, Lochsong has overshadowed the middle-distance stars on the big days.

The real Derby

I've mentioned earlier in this book the first Derby I witnessed in the flesh, when Nijinsky won, but the most astonishing performance I've seen in the race was on television in 1965, when the French-trained Sea Bird II came through late to beat Lester Piggott and Meadow Court by two lengths. For a long way Piggott seemed certain to collect the prize on the Irish colt, but Sea Bird's finishing burst was astonishing. It seemed that jockey Pat Glennon had over-estimated his mount's ability, but the favourite's backers need not have worried. Later that year, Sea Bird demolished what was agreed as the best field ever to contest the Prix de l'Arc de Triomphe, finishing clear of most of Europe's top middle-distance horses.

Many other Derby winners remain in the memory. Shergar, of course, for his ten-length win which launched the career of Walter Swinburn – who then, perversely, had to step aside and watch as Lester Piggott took advantage of his suspension to add the Irish Derby to Shergar's victory roll. Lester returned the compliment in the King George, leading and then vacating the fence on the home turn, allowing Swinburn and Shergar through to win at leisure.

Then there was Troy, for a few weeks during the summer of 1979 the complete racehorse, with an emphatic victory at Epsom where he pulled seven lengths clear in just over a furlong. At The Curragh, then at Ascot and finally reverting to ten furlongs at York in the Benson and Hedges International, Troy showed all the virtues. Speed, stamina, adaptability and versatility made him one of the true stars of the modern era.

And then there was 1994. Nostalgia, they say, is not what it used to be; but only days after the event, I was searching around in the memory trying to find a more satisfying race, one which for me boasted all the ingredients of greatness.

The 1994 Derby, you may remember, was the one which finally, by common consent, was taking the Epsom Classic to its lowest ebb. A poor field of non-stayers, they said, hardly anything good enough to win it, and three of the best colts in England weren't even going to be there. The names Alriffa, Hawker's News and Cicerao may in time indeed become bit-players in the folklore of the British Turf, but in the days leading up to the first Wednesday in June they were spoken of almost in awe. They were the three Classic trial winners who were never entered for Epsom. With little confidence in the chances of the favourite Erhaab staying the trip, even though those noted judges trainer John Dunlop and rider Willie Carson seemed totally convinced he would, a total of twenty-four opponents lined up against him, hoping to benefit from any weakness on his part.

What happened in those 150 or so seconds after the gates sprang open will be worthy of endless reruns on video machines around the country. The trials and tribulations of many of the horses and riders in what was by common consent a uniquely rough race caused several jockeys to find themselves out of position during the crucial part of the race as the field turned into the home straight after Tattenham Corner.

Among them was the frustrated Carson, stuck on the inside, a full fifteen lengths back and apparently all but given up by Dunlop whose attention switched to Khamaseen, on whom Lester Piggott had secured his usual radar-guided clear run around the rail. But Khamaseen could find no more acceleration and was by now vainly chasing the Two Thousand Guineas winner Mister Baileys, who had raced into a six-length lead in a brave act of defiance by his jockey Jason Weaver.

Even inside the two-furlong pole, by which time Khamaseen was clearly not going to win, Mister Baileys looked uncatchable. That was until you looked back and saw Colonel Collins bearing down on the leader, with the Sheikh Mohammed colours, never previously carried into the first four Derby places, also closing in the shape of King's Theatre.

Now there was barely a furlong remaining. The course commentator called out that there were just three horses in contention, even as out of the corner of my eye I noticed the stealthy progress along the inside of Erhaab, obviously not going to win, but closing all the same. Carson, with the wisdom of three previous Derby wins to call on, switched Erhaab wide of his three rivals, galvanized him for a final flourish – and astonished the crowd by flying past all three in little more than fifty yards. So emphatic was the win that by the line he'd already been coasting for thirty yards.

The race had the lot. A bold run by a mile Classic winner ebbing away gallantly as the reserves predictably expired. Two top middle-distance performers then flattering to take the main prize before the *coup de grâce* by a true champion. A ride in a thousand by one of racing's greats.

Still, in the light of that epic race, some newspapers the following day referred to the Derby as a race without stars. Those, of course, were to appear in France the following Sunday. They did; and all three were beaten by two local colts in a fifteen-horse field around the unremarkable Chantilly track.

Never mind the Prix du Jockey Club; leave the real Epsom Derby alone. It's our heritage. Anyone can enter. If they didn't, they should not be eligible to run. As for Erhaab's Derby – what a race. What a jockey. What a winner!

Index